SMALL *Oxford* BOOKS

# THE TURF

SMALL *Oxford* BOOKS

# THE TURF

*Compiled by*
ALAN ROSS

Oxford  New York  Toronto  Melbourne
OXFORD UNIVERSITY PRESS
1982

Oxford University Press, Walton Street, Oxford OX2 6DP

London  Glasgow  New York  Toronto
Delhi  Bombay  Calcutta  Madras  Karachi
Kuala Lumpur  Singapore  Hong Kong  Tokyo
Nairobi  Dar es Salaam  Cape Town
Melbourne  Auckland

and associates in
Beirut  Berlin  Ibadan  Mexico City  Nicosia

British Library Cataloguing in Publication Data

The Turf. — (Small Oxford books)
1. Horse-racing — Literary collections
I. Ross, Alan
820'.8'0355   PR1111.R/
ISBN 0-19-214114-7

Library of Congress Cataloging in Publication Data

Main entry under title:
The Turf.—(Small Oxford books)   Includes index
1. Horse-racing—Addresses, essays, lectures
2. Horse-racing—Literary collections
3. English literature.   I. Ross, Alan
SF335.5.T87   798.4   81-16992
ISBN 0-19-214114-7   AACR2

Set by Western Printing Services Ltd.
Printed in Great Britain by
Hazell Watson & Viney Limited
Aylesbury, Bucks

# *Introduction*

Anyone compiling an anthology about the Turf soon learns that, after cricket, there is more good writing about racing than on any other sport. I do not know why this should be so, unless, perhaps, it is because the Turf involves the whole of society, from the very top to the very bottom, in a particular way. Also, racing is generally conducted in agreeable surroundings, the town in its finery brought to the country. It is not surprising that so many painters have been attracted to the grace and dignity of the parade, the colours of the silks, the variety and excitement of the enclosures, the beauty and nobility of the horses. Racing has an ancient lineage, reflected in its writing.

A racecourse is a place of high hopes and cruel disappointments. It is, all the same, a genial place, shared briefly by millionaires and stable-boys, aristocrats and artisans, in which the great masters of their art – trainers and jockeys – rub shoulders with the unsuccessful, in which high fashion stalks amongst the poorest. Race crowds are lively and good-humoured, addicts of a similar passion, some expert, some happy enough for a day out. Whether they gamble for high or for low stakes they experience in the course of a few minutes similar agonies and delights.

I have tried in this anthology to convey some of racing's excitement and some of its history, to show it from the inside as well as the way it has seemed to develop to the casual visitor. The great characters of the Turf move among tipsters and touts. That is how it should be. From racing's earliest days to the present I have picked up a few themes, selected some key characters. Much, necessarily, has been left out, but here are administrators, owners, trainers, jockeys, bookmakers. Something, too, on the great all-rounders of racing, on the arts of jockeyship and training; on legendary races and famous racehorses; some poetry and fiction. In the background are the movement of crowds, the rustle of silks, the gleam of flanks, the swish of manes and tails, the drumming of horses' hooves, the fresh air of the gallops, the bustle of stables, the thrill of the finish. The racing writer has it all around him.

Editing an anthology of this kind should be a process of self-education. It has certainly been so in this instance. My own credentials – apart from backing horses for thirty years and owning them, under both Rules, for fifteen – were previously little more than derived from a lifetime's scrutiny of *Ruff's Guide to the Turf*, *Raceform*, and *The Sporting Life*. These publications have many merits, but they are as Wisden to the cricketer. They have to do with facts and form, not literature. Acquainting myself with the literature of the Turf has been the real reward.

A.R.

While the snaffle holds, or the long-neck stings,
While the big beam tilts, or the last bell rings,
While horses are horses to train and to race,
Then women and wine take a second place . . .

Rudyard Kipling, 'Song of the G. R.', from
*The Broken Link Handicap*

# Racing & Racegoers

I do not say that all those who go racing are rogues and vagabonds, but I do say that all rogues and vagabonds seem to go racing.

Sir Abe Bailey, Gimcrack Speech, 1937

If I were to begin life again I would go to the Turf to get my friends. They seem to be the only people who hold together. I don't know why; it may be that each knows something that might hang the other, but the effect is delightful and most peculiar.

Harriet, Lady Ashburton to Lord Houghton

It is nonsense to argue, as some do, that business and sport cannot mix. In another age racing may have been purely a sport. But for a long time it has been an industry, and as an industry it has declined because the administrators of racing have had neither the business experience to run it effectively, or apparently the will or even the desire to bring in that experience for the benefit of racing. You now see before you the spectacle of a once proud sport reduced to utter dependence on public money.

David Robinson, Gimcrack Speech, 1969

Received the 15th day of December 1831 of His Grace the Duke of Wellington and Sir William Knighton Bart, executors of his late Majesty King George Fourth deceased, the sum of one hundred pounds on account of services performed in furnishing early racing Intelligence, being in full of all demands.

Ruff

It is forty-seven years since as a lad I went into stables. Three years ago, when I was forcibly returned by the tax inspector who needed our stables to pay death duties, I was still a stable lad, still in the lowest rank, still sneeringly referred to as a 'stable rat'.

Philip Welsh, *Stable Rat*, 1979

Racing belongs to the people. Not to the Jockey Club, not to the owners, especially not to the breeders and not to Old Etonians.

Phil Bull, submission to the Royal Commission on Gambling, 1977 [*63 per cent of the Jockey Club are Old Etonians*]

Racing is just like dram-drinking; momentary excitement and wretched intervals; full consciousness of the mischievous effects of the habit and equal difficulty in abstaining from it.

Charles Greville (1794–1865), the diarist, and owner of the classic winners Preserve (1,000 Guineas) and Mango (St Leger) out of the same mare

Henceforth something to live for. Each morning bringing news of the horse, and the hours of the afternoon passing pleasantly, full of thoughts of the evening paper and the gossip of the bar. A bet on a race brings hope into lives which otherwise would be hopeless.

George Moore, *Esther Waters*, 1894

I have seen flowers come in stony places
And kind things done by men with ugly faces,
And the gold cup won by the worst horse at the
    races . . .

John Masefield, *An Epilogue*

I've had to dig my way through the snow to get to stables on Christmas Days. On lovely summer days when other people were driving to the coast, I'd have to go to stables to feed and water horses, and I used to

say to them, 'If it wasn't for you long-faced buggers
I'd be on the beach now'.

Philip Welsh, Stable Rat, 1979

'My God, Hester, you're eighty-odd thousand to the
good, and a poor devil of a son to the bad. But, poor
devil, poor devil, he's best gone out of a life where he
rides his rocking-horse to find a winner.'

D. H. Lawrence, The Rocking-Horse Winner, 1934

Cicely Lambton thinks that everybody ought to give up
everything except racing, which (she tells me) has
ceased to be a sport and become an industry, and that
everyone should enlist at once except George because
the whole of Cambridgeshire depends on George con-
tinuing his industrial career at Newmarket, and where,
(she asks) should we be at a time like this without
Cambridgeshire?

Raymond Asquith, in a letter to Lady Diana Manners,<br>August 1914

A judge vastly surprised spectators by putting up the
number of the horse that carried a red jacket, when
there seemed no sort of doubt that it had finished some
distance behind the bearer of a green. Up, however,
went the number of the red.

'What did that win by?' a friend of the man in the
box asked him, as he descended to face a wondering
crowd.

'Oh, a good neck,' he replied, adding in a murmur
to his friend, '*The first winner I've backed this week!*'

From The Racing World and Its Inhabitants,<br>ed. Alfred Watson, 1904

The first fine care in training horses for running, and
hunters and hacks for hard riding, is, to train their legs
to be able to carry their carcase; using them first to
short exercise, short gallops, short sweats, and giving

time between their work for their sinews to rest or the best of legs will become destroyed.

Horses' legs are very soon destroyed at first coming into work; but when they have had time to be well trained, scarce any running or riding will hurt them.

Samuel Chifney, *Genius Genuine*, 1804

Horse races and wildgoose chases, which are disports of greater men, and good in themselves, though many gentlemen by such means gallop themselves out of their fortunes.

Robert Burton, *The Anatomy of Melancholy*, 1621

He attended to his game commonly, and didn't much meddle with the conversation except when it was about horses and betting.

William Makepeace Thackeray, *Vanity Fair*, 1847–8

We returned over Newmarket Heathe, the way being mostly a sweet turfe and down, the jockies breathing their fine banks and racers, and giving them their heates.

John Evelyn (1620–1706), *Diary*

# The Racehorse

When mares with foal at foot flee down the glades
Dorothy Wellesley, *Horses*

*By common consent Flying Childers (1715) was the first great racehorse. His sire was The Darley Arabian, from whom, with the Byerley Turk and the Godolphin Arabian, all modern thoroughbreds descend in the male line. There has always been controversy about the breeding of the dam of Flying Childers, but if the* General Stud Book *version is accepted, then Flying Childers stems entirely from imported Eastern horses. Curiously, he only ran twice, in matches at Newmarket, but in a trial against Fox, a leading contemporary, in 1722, Flying Childers gave a stone and won by an estimated distance of 360 yards. It seems to have been evidence enough.*

*Eclipse, foaled nearly fifty years later, was the second in a line of great horses that stretches over 265 years to Shergar, winner of the 1981 Derby. Indifferently bred, Eclipse was never beaten. He is described thus in the* Biographical Encyclopaedia of British Flat Racing:

He had a high-quality, Arab-like profile, great depth through the body and powerful but beautifully moulded quarters. He stood 15 hands 3 at the withers, but a remarkable aspect of his conformation was that the top of his quarters was higher than his withers. This gave him exceptional hip to hock length and the hind-leg leverage which was probably the principal source of his amazing speed. His speed, allied to his indomitable spirit, made him invincible, while his ferocity and his thick-windedness, which caused him to puff and roar as he galloped, made him a formidable animal altogether.

> Full many a daintie horse had he in stable
>
> Chaucer, *Canterbury Tales*, c.1387

*Not long afterwards, in 1780, the first Epsom Derby was run (one year later than the race for fillies, the Oaks). From now on the standard of excellence was set by the winner of that race, the first of which was Diomed, who, after a failure at stud in England, was exported to Virginia to become one of the greatest sires in American history, surpassed only by his descendent Lexington, foaled in 1850 and leading stallion fourteen years in succession.*

*For the most complete expression of the poetry of the horse, and of its courtship, we have to go back to Shakespeare and* Venus and Adonis *(1593). Here are some verses from it.*

His ears up-prick'd; his braided hanging mane
Upon his compass'd crest now stand on end;
His nostrils drink the air, and forth again,
As from a furnace, vapours doth he send:
   His eye, which scornfully glisters like fire,
   Shows his hot courage and his high desire.

Sometime he trots, as if he told the steps,
With gentle majesty and modest pride;
Anon he rears upright, curvets and leaps,
As who should say, 'Lo! thus my strength is tried;
   And this I do to captivate the eye
   Of the fair breeder that is standing by.'

\*     \*     \*

Look, when a painter would surpass the life,
In limning out a well-proportion'd steed,
His art with nature's workmanship at strife,
As if the dead the living should exceed;

[6]

So did this horse excel a common one,
In shape, in courage, colour, pace and bone.

Round-hoof'd, short-jointed, fetlocks shag and long,
Broad breast, full eye, small head, and nostril wide,
High crest, short ears, straight legs and passing strong,
Thin mane, thick tail, broad buttock, tender hide:
  Look, what a horse should have he did not lack
  Save a proud rider on so proud a back.

Sometimes he scuds far off, and there he stares;
Anon he starts at stirring of a feather;
To bid the wind a base he now prepares,
And whe'r he run or fly they know not whether;
  For through his mane and tail the high wind sings,
  Fanning the hairs, who wave like feather'd wings.

\*　　\*　　\*

Then, like a melancholy malcontent,
He vails his tail that, like a falling plume
Cool shadow to his melting buttock lent:
He stamps, and bites the poor flies in his fume.
  His love, perceiving how he is enrag'd,
  Grew kinder, and his fury was assuag'd.

*Earlier still, in 1496, Wynken de Worde established the
fifteen points of a good horse :*

A good horse sholde have three propyrtees of a man,
three of a woman, three of a foxe, three of a hare, and
three of an asse.

> *Of a man.* Bolde, prowde, and hardye.
> *Of a woman.* Fayre-breasted, faire of haire, and
>   easy to move.
> *Of a foxe.* A fair taylle, short eers, with a good
>   trotte.
> *Of a hare.* A grate eye, a dry head, and well
>   rennynge.

*Of an asse.* A bygge chynn, a flag legge, and a good hoof.

*No prospective purchaser, at a bloodstock sale today, would quarrel with any of these requirements.*

*John Welcome has expressed the opinion that Adam Lindsay Gordon's 'How We Beat the Favourite' is 'almost certainly the best racing poem ever written'. Of its twenty-five verses here are the last two :*

On still past the gateway she strains in the straightway,
Still struggles The Clown by a short neck at most:
He swerves, the green scourges; the stand rocks and
    surges,
And flashes, and verges, and flits the white post.

Aye! so ends the tussle – I knew the tan muzzle
Was first, though the ring-men were yelling 'Dead
    Heat!'
A nose I could swear by, but Clarke said 'The mare by
A short head.' And that's how the favourite was beat.

*On the whole I prefer the poems by the Australian 'bush balladeer', A. B. 'Banjo' Paterson, a contemporary of Henry Lawson, who liked to parody him : Paterson wrote numerous racing poems, such as 'The Open Steeplechase'.*

But the pace was so terrific that they soon ran out
    their tether –
They were rolling in their gallop, they were fairly
    blown and beat –
But they both were game as pebbles – neither one
    would show the feather.
And we rushed them at the fences, and they cleared
    them both together,
Nearly every time they clouted, but they somehow
    kept their feet.

*In less rollicking mood he could come up with images of haunting beauty :*

> The champions of the days long fled
> They moved around with noiseless tread,
> Bay, chestnut, brown and black.

*Philip Larkin's celebrated 'At Grass', about Brown Jack, written in the 1950s, nearly a century later, has a similar theme : 'Almanacked, their names live; they | Have slipped their names, and stand at ease, | Or gallop for what must be joy, | And not a fieldglass sees them home . . .' Peter Porter, too, wrote a memorable poem about the Australian wonder horse, Phar Lap. More recently still, in a volume published in 1980, Leslie Norris included fine poems about Ormonde and Hyperion. 'Ormonde' ends*

> . . . Even in age, tendons
> inflexible as bone, blunt clubs
>
> too far from his thinning blood to sense
> the turf, he would not be defeated.
>
> I have to think that natural death
> stood off in awe and would not take
>
> the match on level terms. A bullet
> killed him, smacking into his skull
>
> before the old horse truly knew
> he was under orders. As well he was
>
> unprepared. He would have outrun death.

*More than once, at Ascot or Goodwood, lines from Ezra Pound's poem about a woman 'like a skein of loose silk blown against a wall' who is 'dying piece-meal of a sort of emotional anaemia' have come to me :*

[9]

And round about there is a rabble
Of the filthy, sturdy, unkillable infants of the very poor
They shall inherit the earth

In her is the end of breeding
Her boredom is exquisite and excessive
She would like someone to speak to her
And is almost afraid that I will commit that
    indiscretion.

*The Garden*

*Elsewhere, in 'Near Perigord', Pound conveys something
of the real poetry of riding :*

Bewildering spring, and by the Auvezere
Poppies and day's eyes in the green *émail*
Rose over us; and we knew all that stream
And our two horses had traced out the valleys
Knew the low flooded lands squared out with poplars,
In the young days when the deep sky befriended.

From *Selected Poems*, 1940

*The novels of Nat Gould, despite their sentimentality, give
a real feeling of the racecourse, race riding, and race
preparation. In* The Double Event *the regular jockey is
chloroformed in the paddock by an unscrupulous rival –*

*'Great Heavens! They've hocussed him, and it's only twenty minutes before the race' – and his place is taken by the old grey-haired stud groom who, needless to say, rides Caloola, on whom his master's fate depends, to a thrilling victory. Here is Gould on the paddock at Flemington just before the Melbourne Cup. It shows that he knew what he was doing. Ike is the stud groom, Wells the about to be 'hocussed' jockey.*

Ike had arrived with Caloola, and Wells was also there. The horse looked a perfect picture. His coat shone like satin, and his condition could not be found fault with. And yet there was something about him good judges did not like. 'Short of a winding-up gallop,' said some, and he did look a shade on the big side. However, as he walked slowly about the paddock there was no sign of lameness, but he had his fore-hoof bound up tightly, and a bar-shoe on. Storey was there attending to his charge, and many were the anxious questions he had to answer. Caloola seemed to have lost his bad temper, for he took the attention of the crowd remarkably well. He seemed to know, with that intelligence always to be found in the blood horse, that something great was expected from him that day. His sagacious eyes fairly sparkled and showed the indomitable spirit within. And he would need it all today. The great cracks of the season were to run against him, and he had to give weight to some first-class old horses. Such a field of really good racehorses had not been seen at Flemington for years. No wonder people were excited, and as the time approached for the great race to be decided the crowd surged madly about in all directions. First one rumour and then another was set afloat. Corisande had gone back in the betting. There had been a great rush on Wild Dyrell. Tarana had been knocked out. Chorister was started merely for 'sweep money'. Rainbow was under a cloud. Caloola showed symptoms of lameness again. Euchre was the mount of Power, and so on. What were the public to back? If a man had a fancy, he was put on to something else before he backed it. Every horse in the race carried some money, and there were twenty starters on the board yet. Some men had 'gone for' half a dozen, others for two or three, and very few for a 'single'.

From *The Double Event*

*The horses in Roy Campbell's 'Horses on the Camargue' are not racehorses but his description of them has a muscular virility that could certainly apply to them. The poem ends:*

With white tails smoking free
Long streaming manes, and arching necks, they show
Their kinship to their sisters of the sea –
And forward hurl their thunderbolts of snow.
Still out of hardship bred
Spirits of power and beauty and delight
Have ever on such frugal pastures fed
And loved to course with tempests through the night.

From *Adamastor*, 1930

# The Jockey Club

*The Jockey Club, neither a club in the Johnsonian sense, nor an association of jockeys, has ruled British racing since the middle of the eighteenth century. The three men who, in their different ways, did most to establish the Jockey Club's status as the arbiter of all Turf matters, were Sir Charles Bunbury, Lord George Bentinck, and Admiral Rous. The first two were associated in the public mind with the exposure of racing scandals – Bunbury with the 'Escape' affair, Bentinck with Running Rein's Derby switch – and the third published in 1850* The Law and Practice of Horse Racing *and became the greatest authority on handicapping.*

By this time (1767) Sir Charles Bunbury's wife, the beautiful Lady Sarah, had run off with Lord William Gordon. The husband she left behind was rich, respectable, hypochondriac ('he loves to be thought ill –' Lady Sarah Lennox observed to Lady Susan O'Brien) and his name crops up in nearly every aspect of late eighteenth-century racing. He bred Highflyer, owned Gimcrack, and won the first Derby.

He was not among the members who registered their colours in 1762: he was only 22 at the time. He was a member soon afterwards. He was not interested in travel, politics, the arts or women. Like Tregonwell Frampton he liked coursing. Like him he lived for the Turf. Other great racing men of his day had other concerns: Grafton, Rockingham, Derby, and March ('Old Q') who *was* interested in women. Not Bunbury. His single-mindedness, rectitude and courage gave the

Jockey Club a moral authority which, in the nineteenth century, it sometimes conspicuously lacked. He became 'Perpetual President'. He was the third dictator of the Turf (following Charles II and Frampton), and the first whose *cathedra* was the Club (preceding Bentinck and Rous).

Roger Longrigg, *The History of Horse Racing*, 1972

*Bunbury died in 1821. 'What the Turf got in the 1840s,' writes Longrigg, 'was an autocrat of immense energy but questionable morals.'*

*About Bentinck his cousin Charles Greville, the diarist, wrote in 1848,*

Oh for the inconsistency of human nature, the strange compound and medley of human motives and impulses, when the same man who crusaded against the tricks and villainies of others did not scruple to do things quite as bad as the worst of the misdeeds which he so vigorously and unrelentingly attacked.

*Bentinck was an unscrupulous gambler on a vast scale, an arrogant and successful owner who won seven Classics (including the 2,000 Guineas, the 1,000 Guineas, and the Oaks in 1840 with the same horse, Crucifix), an MP who led the Protectionist Party, and an outstanding Turf reformer, especially in his concern for ordinary racegoers and his war on crooks. He invented the flag start, developed Goodwood as a racecourse, and died on the verge of a great political career at the age of 46.*

*Of Admiral Henry John Rous, the last of the great Turf dictators,* British Flat Racing *observes 'he formed the link between the rough and ready racing of the early nineteenth century and the highly organized sport that we know today'. Rous's greatest achievements were in the realms of administration and handicapping. He wrote in his* Law and Practice of Horse Racing:

A public handicapper should be a man of independent circumstances, in every sense of the word, and beyond suspicion of accepting illicit compensation for favours received; attached to no stable, a good judge of the condition of the horse, but with a more intimate knowledge of the dispositions of owners and trainers, he should be a spectator of every race of any importance in the United Kingdom; and his station should be at the distance-post, where horses are pulled, not at the winning post, where they are extended; he should never make a bet, and he should treat all the remarks which may be made about his handicaps with the utmost indifference.

*Advocating the appointment of a public handicapper Rous wrote in a letter to the Press:*

We want a man, like Caesar's wife, above suspicion, of independent means, a perfect knowledge of the form and actual condition of every public horse, without

[15]

having the slightest interest in any stable. If by any possibility you can find this man above price, he would throw up his office in three months, disgusted with many horse-owners, whose sole knowledge of racing is confined to running horses for stakes, and abusing the handicappers.

[He was called] 'the Great Master of Weights'. He knew from his own observation the condition of the runners, and every little thing that he thought might militate for or against the chance any horse had of winning he was no stranger to; carefully noting the same in a book for further reference as often as necessity required; an object he undoubtedly thought too important to trust even to the strongest memory. An instance I can give, and a strong one, in support of this fact.

When St Giles was entered in a Handicap at Ascot as a two-year-old, in 1856, the Admiral to my thinking, and to the late Lord Ribblesdale's mind (the owner of the horse), had very greatly over-estimated his capabilities, by putting a much heavier weight on him than his running justified, the sole test by which the merits of all horses can be judged. On being asked his reasons for doing so he said, 'I don't know, but will look'; and on referring to his notes in the book I have mentioned, replied laconically – 'Fat, Ribblesdale, fat'.

William Day, *Turf Celebrities I Have Known*, 1891

His great delight was in handicapping. 'There,' he exclaimed once, after finishing his labours in connection with one of the big races, 'there, now none of them can win!' As a very old man he complained that he found great difficulty in finding his way from his house to his club, in London; 'but', he exclaimed, 'I can still handicap'.

D. W. E. Brock, *The Racing Man's Weekend Book*

*Rous died, aged 82, in 1877. In the hundred years since his death the Jockey Club has, sometimes with considerable reluctance, been obliged to make many changes that would have been unthinkable at its inauguration. It has remained an essentially upper-class institution, but the creation of the Levy Board has reduced its economic independence. In 1966 the first woman, Mrs Florence Nagle, was granted a training licence, in 1973 women were allowed to race against men in amateur races, and two years later they were allowed to become professional. In 1977 the first women members of the Jockey Club were elected.*

# Bookmakers & Betting

Betting is the manure to which the enormous crop of horse-racing and racehorse breeding in this and other countries is to a large extent due.

R. Black, *The Jockey Club and Its Founders*, 1891

Speed and accuracy are the essentials of a tic-tac man. A backer may have made careful plans to put a lot of money on a certain horse, spreading it among many bookies in the various rings: he hopes, by employing a number of people to make his bets for him, to get all his money on without causing the odds to shorten. But he may reckon without the tic-tac man, by whose help the news of the very first bet is flashed around the bookies, causing them almost instantaneously to shorten their odds. And, accuracy: it is recorded that one tic-tac man flicked a fly off his nose and thereby cost his employer a king's ransom.

D. W. E. Brock, *The Racing Man's Weekend Book*, 1949

From 1843 the visible ring was to an extent cleaned up, and a new phenomenon appeared: the big bookmaker

[18]

who was honest. The most famous were Fred Swindell and 'Leviathan' Davies. Swindell was born a Devonshire labourer, and became an engine-cleaner at the age of twelve. He took his savings racing and preferred the life. He walked to London, and by dint of sobriety, discretion, and intelligence succeeded as a commissioner and lawyer. He worked for the greatest owners like James Merry, the uncouth Glasgow ironmaster, and Sir Joseph Hawley, the 'lucky baronet'. He is said to have gone to live next door to Admiral Rous in order to see who called on him. He died very rich.

Roger Longrigg, *The History of Horse Racing*, 1972

*Charles Dickens is described in Forster's life of him as having, in the novelist's words, 'a wonderful paralyzing coincidence' at Doncaster one Leger day.*

He bought the card, facetiously wrote down three names as the winners of the three chief races (never in his life having heard or thought of any of the horses, except that of the winner of the Derby, who proved to be nowhere). In a letter to his biographer he says: 'If you can believe it, without your hair standing on end, those three races were won one after another by those three horses!'

The firm of Peach & Steel were amongst the leviathans of their day, and they started from small beginnings. At one time they were a small firm on the racecourse, and were satisfied to make £100 'Books'. One day they went to the Wye races, expecting to trade on their usual scale. As luck would have it, Lord Hastings, who subsequently fell foul of Henry Chaplin, and died a penniless man, was present at the meeting, and on Peach & Steel offering 'evens on the field', booked an 'even thousand' against his fancy, and on the day lost £10,000 to the firm – and, what is more to the point, paid it.

[19]

Peach & Steel at that time were not a wealthy firm, but from that day they never looked back. Many firms can trace their success to a lucky start like this. Jack Burns has cause to bless the late Lord Wilton, who is reported to have lost £30,000 to him; Douglas Stuart similarly had a lucky 'touch' from a millionaire's son; Patsy Cadogan once had £10,000 to £1,000 laid on a loser by a certain Royal Highness; Ernest Benzon (the 'Jubilee Plunger') laid the foundations of another book-maker's fortune, and similar instances could be quoted almost *ad nauseam*.

Thomas Henry Day, *Leaves from a Bookmaker's Book*, 1910

Lord Hippo suffered fearful loss
By putting money on a horse
Which he believed, if it were pressed,
Would run far faster than the rest.

Hilaire Belloc, *More Peers*

I have heard of riding wagers
Where horses have been nimbler than the sands.

William Shakespeare, *Cymbeline*

*In the end, of course, quantitatively if not qualitatively, the Turf belongs not to owners, breeders, trainers, jockeys, but to punters. Betting for the vast majority is what it's all about, and while winning is one thing, getting the money safely home is quite another. Ras Prince Monolulu, the great racecourse tipster, wrote in his autobiography* I Gotta Horse (*1950*):

Winners in those days were always marked men. If they were able to get away from the course with the money they were followed all the way back to town, and if they still had it when they got off the train at Waterloo or Victoria they were lucky men. If they even got as far as the station they were fortunate. But the

'boys' always had it back. I've known a punter leave
Bath racecourse clutching his winnings in his pocket,
get to the station, hang on to his money to Paddington,
jump on a bus in Praed Street, and before he's got to
Marble Arch he's had his pocket cut right out of his
trousers – pants and all! All his winnings gone with the
wind! And if he didn't lose it that way and the gangs
working with the bookmakers couldn't take it by 'fair'
means, there was always the 'cosh'.

*In the same book 'Prince' Monolulu describes the methods
of the old bookies and their accomplices when a big winner
came up to collect. The bookie, Monolulu observes, would
remain 'as calm as a mermaid sitting on a block of ice'.*

'Here you are, sir. It's a pleasure to pay you. Twenty
to one to ten pounds, wasn't it, sir? That's right, Harry,
it's in the book. Stand away there, you'll all get paid,
but this gentleman has a large sum to come and I must
pay him out first. Now, sir. Ten, twenty, thirty, fifty,
eighty, one hundred. And here's another twenty, forty,
fifty, two hundred, and your ten pounds back. Thank
you, sir. There you are, ladies and gentlemen. Billie
always pays, no matter whether it's ten shillings or two
hundred pounds. Hold it up high, sir. Let the ladies
and gentlemen see that your money is safe with Billie.'
The bookie lifts the backer's arms, holds them high
above his head so that the crowd can see the hands
clasping the fat wad of notes.

Then, like a summer thunderstorm coming from out
of the clouds, another hand flashes out from the crowd,
whisks away the money out of the backer's hands, and
all he is left with is 'Oh, bad luck, sir! You really should
have been more careful. Now here we are, large prices.
Six to four the field. Roll up with your bets. What's
that, sir? Of course I've paid you. If you can't look
after your money when you've got it, you mustn't

expect me to act as the Bank of England for you. Six to four the field.' And on the train back to town the bookie collects his two hundred back, leaving the odd tenner for his smart-Alec accomplice.

*There has always been, in certain quarters, moral disapproval of horse-racing and gambling. After Persimmon won the Derby for the Prince of Wales in 1896 there were whispers – totally unsubstantiated – that the horse had been 'allowed' to win. An article in* Racing Illustrated *thundered back :*

The puritanical Pharisees who day by day thank their God that they are not as other men are, and who in the narrow-minded circles of their own little Bethels preach and prate against the doings of far better men than themselves, having lifted up their voices, have met, and passed resolutions under high sounding titles, whose length is inversely proportioned to their importance, calling upon the Prince to sever his connections with the Turf; which latter they are pleased to term 'the great national engine of gambling'.

It is the same old story. A lot of conceited, self-advertising nobodies see a chance of getting their names in print, and becoming of some importance in their own little locality; therefore, regardless whether men will speak well of them or not, they intrude their bigoted and narrow-minded opinions on the world at large. Some obscure pastor of the Old Tony Weller's 'shepherd' class has addressed a letter of remonstrance to the Prince for participating in a sport which the councils of the nation have legalized, and in which every Englishman worthy of the name is more or less interested.

. . . Naturally they and all the puritanical crew are desperately anxious to draw the Prince of Wales away from the Turf, seeing as they do what a blow his patronage of the national sport has struck at their ridiculous organization. But if there is one thing more than another for which the Prince of Wales has become noted throughout his career, it is for being possessed of sound common sense, and he is not likely to follow the dictation of any man, least of all a man who pursues such very questionable methods of attaining his ends as the secretary of the Anti-Gambling League.

. . . In fact there is no getting away from the impression that the whole thing is a sham, organized by certain people simply for self-advertising purposes. The Anti-Gambling League, the Non-conformist Conscience, and the South London Evangelical Free Church Council are only different developments of our old acquaintances – the immortal Stiggins and Chadband. All said and done, nothing hits off the character of the average 'shepherd' better than the time honoured conversation held between the Dissenting grocer and his apprentice:

'James.' 'Yes Sir!'

'Have you sanded the sugar?' 'Yes Sir.'

'Have you stoned the currants?' 'Yes Sir.'

'Have you watered the rum?' 'Yes Sir.'

'Then come to prayers.'

Quoted in Michael Seth-Smith, *Bred for the Purple*, 1969

The days of the small fiddler – and I don't mean a short man with a violin – with a voice as sweet and low as that of an archbishop and manners and politeness that would put even Mayfair to shame, are over, gone for ever. True, we still see them occasionally trying to break the five-furlong record at Lewes or Ascot, or some of the other wide open spaces, but those accommodating gentlemen who allow a backer who has put £2 on with them the opportunity of seeing a race in comfort – 'Come up here and stand on my box, sir, you'll see better' – and then, like the Arab, steal silently away, are in a great minority.

From *Sporting Stories* by 'Thormanby', 1909

# Derby Day

This day there is a great throng to Banstead Downs upon a great horse-race.

Samuel Pepys (1633–1703), Diary

Last year it was iced champagne, claret cup and silk overcoats; now it ought to be hot brandy and water, foot baths and flannels.

Charles Dickens, after the Derby of 1863

A day of extraordinary excitement and interest to the sportsman, and to millions of others in every part of England, from the manufacturers of twelve stories high to the Yorkshire ploughman; from the cockney behind his counter to the cellarman at Hatchetts.

> Benjamin Marshall (1768–1835), painter and journalist, who moved to Newmarket in 1812 because 'the second animal in creation is a fine horse and at Newmarket I can study him in the greatest grandeur, beauty and variety'.

*In 1979 the Derby was run for the 200th time, an occasion celebrated by a magnificent exhibition at the Royal Academy, which included works by the Alkens, Degas, Doré, Dufy, Fabergé, Frith, Gainsborough, Gericault, Herring, Lavery, Millais, Munnings, J. N. Sartorius, Stubbs and others.*

Such tragic scenes I saw on the course . . . a woman crying bitterly, evidently a paramour of the man who was languidly lolling on the cushions flushed with drink, and trying to look unconcerned at the woman's grief. This was probably caused by a notice that his losses that day obliged him to do without her society for the future.

Sir John Millais, 31 May 1853 in a letter to Charles Collins

The acrobats with every variety of performance, the nigger minstrels, gipsy fortune-telling, to say nothing of carriages filled with pretty women, together with the sporting element . . . the more I considered the kaleidoscopic aspect of the crowd on Epsom Downs, the more firm became my resolve to reproduce it.

W. P. Frith, *My Autobiography and Reminiscences*, 1887

*Fortunes have been spent by millionaires on trying to win the Derby. Yet, curiously, a few men have won it several times: Lord Egremont and the Aga Khan five times, J. Bowes, Sir J. Hawley, the 1st Duke of Westminster and Sir Victor Sassoon four times, and nine others three times. Many famous trainers have never won the Derby, yet three, Robson, Porter, and F. Darling, won it seven times each, M. Dawson won it six times, and nine others three times or more.*

*The same is largely true of jockeys. Sir Gordon Richards, champion jockey twenty-six times, finally won a Derby at the twenty-eighth attempt at the age of 49 (on Pinza in 1953). Yet Lester Piggott, who won it first in 1954 at the age of 18, went on to win it seven more times by 1980. J. Robinson and S. Donoghue won it six times (Donoghue three times in succession, and four times out of five between 1921 and 1925), J. Arnull, F. Archer and W. Clift won it five times each.*

*Perhaps the Derby of 1880 was the most extraordinary of all, bringing together a legendary horse, Bend Or, and a legendary jockey, Fred Archer. Here is part of John Welcome's account of it:*

Bend Or was a magnificent chestnut colt standing over sixteen hands, all of them quality, with an odd round black mark on his near quarter said to have been about the size of a tennis ball. He was a splendid example of the thoroughbred in every way, kind and gentle in the stable and the paddock, genuine and gallant on the racecourse. Robert Peck had owned his sire, Doncaster, for which he had paid £10,000; later he had persuaded the Duke of Westminster to give him the vast sum for those days of 14,000 guineas for the stallion. Peck believed Bend Or could win the Derby, vindicate his judgement and show that the money spent for the sire had not been thrown away. Naturally he wanted the best rider he could get, and that, in his judgement, was Archer. Lord Falmouth's runner, Apollo, was not of much account. He agreed to release Archer from his first claim. The engagement of Archer to ride Bend Or was accordingly announced to the Press as definite.

*But soon after Archer was badly savaged by a colt, and one arm left torn and mutilated.*

Peck and the Duke were faced with an appallingly difficult decision. Arm or no arm Archer declared that he was fit to ride Bend Or and that he had the right to do so. Whether he could in fact do justice to the horse was something on which trainer and owner had to make up their minds. The decision was made even more difficult than usual this particular year since it was clear from the form that Bend Or was going to have to run for his life if he were to win and that a close and hard-fought finish could be expected.

There was one other colt of very high class indeed in the field. This was Mr Charles Brewer's Robert the Devil trained by Manton who had a half share in him and who had engaged Tom Cannon to ride him. . . .

Bend Or did not have a race before the Derby. He developed sore shins and, as with Archer's arm, they refused to respond properly to treatment. None the less, because of his two-year-old form, which was brilliant, and Peck's known opinion of him as one of the best he had ever had, he was made and stayed favourite for the race. . . .

Robert the Devil's connections were having their troubles, too. Tom Cannon was unexpectedly claimed to ride Mr Gretton's Mariner. All the other leading jockeys were engaged so Manton had to replace Cannon with Rossiter who was never better than second rate. This may explain why Robert the Devil drifted in the betting and started only third favourite at the price of 7–1, though it was said that his owners backed him heavily even with Rossiter on him.

It was fortunate that Bend Or had the placid temperament of the really great racehorse on the big occasion. . . .

The same could not be said for his rider. Knowing the responsibility which rested upon him he was even more strung up than usual. He had had to get his weight down by a stone in the last few days before the race and had done it by a regimen of violent purgation and dosing with 'the mixture' that far exceeded even his usual extreme measures. 'I shall sit in the Turkish Bath and no doubt elsewhere,' he once told Dawson and Portland when, on another occasion he had to get weight off in a hurry. This is what he had done right up to Derby day and it had left him weak, nervy and irritable. His arm, though not as bad as has been sometimes said, was nevertheless all but useless and would certainly be of no help to him in a finish. It was not in a sling as many have described it but there was a pad in his palm and a piece of iron bound to the arm inside the jacket. Lunching off a crumb of a biscuit and a sip of champagne, testy with everyone who came near him during the morning, he was a mass of nerves when he was lifted into the saddle. . . .

The race was run faster than usual in those days and Tattenham Corner was sharper then than it is now. Archer had reason to swear and cause for worry. Owing to his shins Bend Or's action was not right and he did

not come down the hill at all well. He was in danger of losing his place and what is more he was being crowded. Yet he would yield the inside to nobody. At the turn the field was right on top of him, the air was thick with curses, and his were the loudest. He was so close to the rails that to get around at all he had to lift the nearer of his long legs on to Bend Or's withers. Thus began the legend that he rode his Derbys with one leg over the rails. It has been said of others since then but it was first said of him and it was Bend Or's Derby that began it.

Robert the Devil had opened up a long lead and in the straight he increased it. No one believed that he could be caught. The crowd were yelling him home and the bookmakers freely calling for ten to one on him.

Then Archer balanced Bend Or and began his run. The lack of an arm at this stage made little difference to his immense strength, his horsemanship and his ability to impart his own driving force to the horse. Bend Or responded to him with a courage equal to his own. The gap began to close. The cheering for Robert the Devil suddenly ceased and the bookmakers' voices fell away. Within the last furlong Bend Or was there with a chance but it was only that for the task he had been set appeared too great. A hundred yards from the post Archer, forgetting his useless arm, went for his whip and dropped it. But he wouldn't give in. Nor would his horse.

Then Rossiter, mesmerized perhaps by the thought of Archer behind him and the thunder of hooves bearing down on him, committed that most fatal of all errors. He looked around and, unbalanced, Robert the Devil faltered. Against Archer no one could afford the misjudgement even of an instant. In these last few seconds he saw his chance of victory and seized it. He called on Bend Or for one final effort. It seemed to the onlookers that his long legs almost lifted Bend Or level with the leader. Bend Or responded to him and stretched his stride. The two horses, locked together, came past the post.

No one could say with certainty which of them had won. . . . Then the numbers went up and it was seen that No. 7, Bend Or, was first in the frame. He had won by a head. . . .

Bend Or owes the fact that his name appears amongst the winners for the Derby to two things – his courage and Archer's strength and opportunism. The feat of riding this superb finish without a whip and with the use of only one arm has never been equalled in the annals of race-riding and horsemanship. To make the achievement even greater they found after the race that Bend Or had spread a plate during it.

John Welcome, *Fred Archer*, 1967

*Well might Archer remark to an American reporter later on, 'My most sensational victory? The Derby on Bend Or. It was right out of the fire I can tell you, sir.'*

*Of all nineteenth-century novels in which racing and gambling play a part, in none are they so much worked into the main theme as in George Moore's Esther Waters,*

*published in 1894. Esther Waters is a completely natural-
istic description of the seduction of a servant-girl; slum
life in London, Soho pubs, Plymouth Brethren, bookmakers are all part of a moving, low-keyed love story set
among gamblers. Its great set piece is Derby Day, in which
Moore produces the literary equivalent of Frith's famous
painting. The race itself – though its preliminaries and
bookmaking activities are lengthily discussed – is scarcely
mentioned, for the scenes on the Downs, the gypsies and
roundabouts, occupy Esther's attention so fully that she
misses the finish. In closely observed passages Moore describes people pouring on to the course and afterwards
drifting away in the late afternoon.*

A vast crowd swarmed over the opposite hill, and
beyond the crowd the women saw a piece of open
downland dotted with bushes, and rising in a gentle
incline to a belt of trees which closed the horizon.
'Where them trees are, that's *Tattenham Corner*.' The
words seemed to fill old John with enthusiasm, and he
described how the horses came round this side of the
trees. 'They comes right down that 'ere 'ill – there's the
dip – and they finishes opposite to where we is standing. Yonder, by Barnard's Ring.'

'What, all among the people?' said Sarah.

'The police will get the people right back up the
hill.'

'That's where we shall find William,' said Esther.

'I'm getting a bit peckish; ain't you, dear? He's got
the luncheon basket. But, lor', what a lot of people!
Look at that.'

What had attracted Sarah's attention was a boy
walking through the crowd on a pair of stilts fully eight
feet high. He uttered short warning cries from time to
time, held out his wide trousers and caught pennies in
his comical hat. Drags and carriages continued to arrive.

The sweating horses were unyoked, and grooms and helpers rolled the vehicles into position along the rails. Lackeys drew forth cases of wine and provisions, and the flutter of table-cloths had begun to attract vagrants, itinerant musicians, fortune-tellers, begging children. All these plied their trades round the fashion of grey frock-coats and silk sunshades. All along the rails rough fellows lay asleep with their hats over their faces, clay pipes sticking from under their brims, their brown-red hands upon the grey grass.

*While the race is actually being run Esther and her friend Sarah are riding wooden horses on a merry-go-round.*

Round and round they went, their steeds bobbing nobly up and down to the sound of fifes, drums and cymbals. They passed the winning-post many times; they had to pass it five times and the horse that stopped nearest it won the prize. A long drawn-out murmur, continuous as the sea, swelled up from the course – a murmur which at last passed into words: 'Here they come; blue wins, the favourite's beat.' Esther paid little attention to these cries; she did not understand them;

they reached her indistinctly and soon died away, absorbed in the strident music that accompanied the circling horses. These had now begun to slacken speed . . . They went slower and slower.

§

Derby Day was one of the hottest in memory and the crowds on the Downs sizzled in the sunshine on the last day of May. Many of them thought that they were melting away in the heat and wondered how much of them would be left to see the sunset. One spectator noted that 'there were fat women in purple satin with ostrich feathers in their bonnets, babies galore in traps with their fathers blowing cornets and drinking stout. There were road-side tables laiden with lemonade in tumblers, and ice-cold "coolers". There were tramps, walking parties, cyclists and one-legged men on crutches. Blue clouds of petrol fumes contaminated the air. Trees bandaged with posters advertising soap, newspapers and chocolate, and giving news of the execution of the poisoner Armstrong. Other posters screamed "Anxiety about Pondoland".'

*That passage from* Steve (*1974*) *by Michael Seth-Smith, describes the scene on the day Donoghue won the Derby for the second year in succession, a feat not accomplished since Danny Maher did it twenty years earlier.*

Thrapston led, with Hyperion chasing him, and hugging the inside rail. Rounding the Tattenham turn, Donoghue glanced over his left shoulder, quickly deciding that he had neither the right nor the incentive to block the forward move of his imminent challenge. It was Hyperion's Derby from then on . . .

Tears impelled by the drama of the occasion; the vast roaring of applause from the crowd on the Downs; the cheering from well-wishers thronging the rails;

slaps on the back from Lord Lonsdale and fellow-members of the Jockey Club; and, from above, the decorous hand-claps and patting of race cards on balustrade by the assembled Royal family.

Yes, indeed, any man would envy Lord Derby's supreme moment as he took the leading rein over from bowler-hatted Bill Newman and steered his cocky little chestnut colt and his grin-happy Yorkshire jockey, Tommy Weston, into that small oval whose short-clipped grasses are transformed, this once-a-year occasion, into plumes of pure emerald.

The blue flag was hoisted on the number-board. The bookies paid out. The owner went upstairs to receive the congratulations from King George V and Queen Mary. Hyperion threw his head up and down as he relished his douching and rubbing-over in a far corner of the paddock. Mrs Lambton, from the Clerk of the Course's office, put a telephone-call through to her husband. And then the champagne-glasses were refilled and quickly emptied as Gordon Richards on Fougasse led the canter to post of the runners for the Stewards' Handicap . . .

From *Hyperion* (1967), ed. Clive Graham, on the 1933 Derby

# Owners

Well, Lord, we trainers can let it be,
Why can't these owners abstain the same?
It can't be aught but a losing game.

John Masefield

Porter told me that the Duke of Westminster visited Kingsclere during the autumn after Ormonde had won the Two Thousand Guineas, Derby, and St Leger, and, much to Porter's surprise, expressed his intention of riding Ormonde at exercise. Porter tried to dissuade him from doing so, but the Duke said, 'I want to ride, and I am accustomed, Mr Porter, to having my own way, so will you kindly have Ormonde brought here.' Porter then added, 'Well, Your Grace, I can take no responsibility for this'; to which the Duke replied, 'Mr Porter, I do not ask you to take any responsibility: is the horse yours or mine? Please have him brought here.' After that there was no more to be said. Not long after this I met the Duke, and asked him about his ride. He said, 'Though I have ridden all my life, it was the most disagreeable experience I ever went through, for when Ormonde started in his gallop he put his head down between his knees, pulling the reins through my hands, and his hind legs were so powerful that I thought I was going to be shot over his head with every stride he took. I sat back as if I were riding over a big fence, and hoped for the best. I knew perfectly well I had no control over the beast at all, and I wondered how I was going to pull him up when the time came. Fortunately for me, when the leading horses slowed down, Ormonde did the same, broke into a trot, and then into a walk.

Then, he made a violent stumble and I very nearly fell over his head. Porter expressed great relief that all had gone off well, and, in my heart of hearts, I really agreed with him, though I did not say so.'

The Duke of Portland, *Memories of Racing and Hunting*, 1935

*The 6th Duke of Portland, who wrote the above in the first of two shrewdly amusing volumes of memoirs published in the 1930s, was the owner of St Simon, possibly the greatest of all English racehorses, whom he bought for 1,600 guineas on the death of his breeder Prince Batthyany. Many of the leading trainers of the time trained for him – Matthew and George Dawson, John Porter, George Lambton, and Fred Darling among others – and in the 1880s and 1890s he won all the classics, including the Derby in successive years. He also imported the Australian horse Carbine, record winner of the 1890 Melbourne Cup, for his Welbeck stud. He wrote touchingly about him in his memoirs :*

Carbine could not bear to get his ears wet, and once, when he was being saddled and bridled to run for the Melbourne Cup, it began to rain. For some time he refused to go out of his box: so, in desperation, his trainer Higginbotham put up an umbrella, and walked to the starting post holding this over the horse's head. When he was at the starting post with the other horses, he paid no further attention to the wet, however – and he won the race. In consequence of this idiosyncrasy Higginbotham had a leather protector made like a small umbrella which he attached to the bridle, so that rain could not fall on Carbine's ears: and this contraption was sent to Welbeck with him.

*The Duke of Portland, one of the true patricians of the Turf, won over £73,000 in 1889 and gave the lot to charity. Not many, before or since, have acted so magnanimously, though several could have afforded it. Eight years*

*later the Duke, with more horses in training, won only one
race worth £490.*

The high proportion of aristocrats among owners led
to a belief in some quarters that owning racehorses was
an accompaniment not just of wealth but of social
position: certainly patronage of local meetings was an
obligation of their place in the social hierarchy and
participation at others a self-imposed requirement of
society's social diary.

Wray Vamplew, The Turf: a social and economic<br>history of horse-racing, 1976

*Since the nineteenth century the pattern has changed;
industrialists, businessmen, successful tradesmen, in
syndicates or on their own, bookmakers and professional
gamblers have all seen ownership of racehorses as a way
of gaining social prestige and making money. Compara-
tively few have succeeded, especially since racing was rid
of its crooks and swindlers, many of them aristocrats.*

Owners and their agents were the biggest cheats,
including, in O'Kelly's view, the Jockey Club dukes.
Matches were fixed, horses were pulled in sweepstakes,
and ringers were run less innocently than by Lord
Egremont.

Roger Longrigg, The History of Horse Racing, 1972

*According to Longrigg some of Lord Egremont's five
Derby winners were probably four-year-olds; so casual
was the running of his stables that horses frequently got
mixed.*

*O'Kelly was a real Turf character. An Irish immigrant,
illiterate, he worked successively as sedan-chairman,
billiards and tennis marker, and beer carrier to his fellow
inmates of the Fleet prison where he spent some time for
failing to pay his debts. Backed by the notorious Charlotte
Hayes he made a fortune out of gambling, purchased a
commission (rising to the rank of lieutenant-colonel), and*

*ended up by buying the great Eclipse for a mere 1,750
guineas. 'Eclipse first, and the rest nowhere,' was his
famous remark after betting he could place the runners of
a heat in correct order. Since Eclipse won by more than a
distance (240 yards) O'Kelly won his bet, the other four
runners all being eliminated.*

*Eclipse was never beaten in eighteen races, earning over
£25,000 in winnings and stud fees. His son Young
Eclipse won the Derby for O'Kelly in 1781, and three
years later O'Kelly won the Derby again with Sergeant.*

*In the nineteenth century great owners came in all shapes
and sizes, mad, eccentric, profligate. Some, like Palmer-
ston, with his red-dyed whiskers, were successful politicians,
others, like James Merry, iron-masters. The 5th Earl of
Rosebery was the first Prime Minister to win the Derby
while in office. John Bowes, a recluse married to a French
actress and the son of Lord Strathmore, won four Derbys
but scarcely ever saw his horses either in their stables or on
the racecourse. Some, like the Marquis of Hastings, and
Jack Mytton, who drank himself to death, were compulsive
losers. None, though, compared in oddness with the Earl
of Glasgow:*

He bred and raced on an immense scale, with unprecedented lack of success. He was reckoned unlucky, but he counted ill-luck as though he loved it. If his opponent's horse was bad, his was worse; if his own horse was good, his opponent's was better. To shrewder men like Bentinck he was a gold-mine. He changed trainers and jockeys as other people changed hats. But his furies and dismissals contained no vindictiveness; he often went back to men he had dismissed. His enormous stud was run on whimsical lines. He was obstinately loyal to certain blood-lines of proved uselessness. Like Sir Tatton Sykes of Sledmere, he refused to give his horses names, which caused confusion. When he was dissatisfied with a horse (as he often had cause to be) he had it shot. The slaughter over the years was appalling. With all this, he inspired great personal affection and loyalty.

Roger Longrigg, *The History of Horse Racing*, 1972

*The Turf has not lacked for variety of characters in recent years amongst its successful (and unsuccessful) owners : kings, queens, sheikhs, actors, playwrights, authors, military men, farmers, hairdressers. Some of these knew a lot, some very little. All, in one way or another, were prey to the excitement of the racecourse. In modern times two of the most publicly identified owners have been the Aga Khan (1877–1957), winner of five Derbys and six St Legers, and Miss Dorothy Paget (1905–60), owner of the legendary Golden Miller, winner of the Grand National and five Cheltenham Gold Cups.*

*Although his activities were not always welcomed by the racing fraternity, the Aga, squat, bespectacled, plump and smiling – a Bombay gentleman from top hat to the tip of his ubiquitous umbrella – was a popular figure to the general public. His Derby win with Bahram confirmed this :*

At the top of the hill Field Trial took up the running,

while behind him came First Son. These two were now clear of the field, and they maintained this advantage as they entered the Straight. Here First Son was beaten, and it seemed then that Field Trial would win the race for Lord Astor. But Bahram quickly showed that he was a force to be reckoned with. Moving effortlessly, the Aga Khan's wonderful and invincible colt simply strode past the leader, and went on with the race won. There could be no manner of doubt about that, although there remained two furlongs to go. The only challenge to his supremacy came, somewhat unexpectedly, from Robin Goodfellow, whose chances in the race had not been much favoured. Coming with a great run, that colt went past Field Trial, but was quite unable to make any sort of impression on Bahram. The Aga Khan's colt passed the winning-post two lengths ahead. It was a very long time since I had seen so easy a victory in such a great race. . . .

Though there had been a stir of excitement among the spectators when it was seen that it was Field Trial who was leading into the Straight, this quickly died away when Bahram took the lead. It was as if everybody was saying to himself: 'He will win. There was never any other possible result.' As a consequence Bahram's great victory was received almost in silence. The popularity of the result was only demonstrated when the Aga Khan, wearing a silk hat and carrying an umbrella, was seen hurrying towards the group of horses and jockeys beyond the paddock. Then the cheers were hearty and prolonged. Afterwards His Majesty King George V sent for the Aga Khan, to congratulate him on his second Derby win. At a subsequent dinner at Buckingham Palace, at which His Highness was the guest of honour, King George proposed the health of the winning owner.

R. C. Lyle, *The Aga Khan's Horses*, 1938

[40]

*Dorothy Paget resembled the Aga Khan possibly only in shape :*

One of the great eccentrics of twentieth-century racing, Miss Paget was inordinately shy, largely through an aversion to men. Usually dressed in a large grey over-coat that came down almost to her ankles and a blue felt hat, she had a round pale face and straight dark hair. To avoid being accosted by strangers, the racing press and almost anybody else, she surrounded herself with a bevy of female secretaries.

During the last twenty years of her life she rarely went racing and lived as a recluse at Chalfont St Giles in Buckinghamshire, consuming gigantic meals at all hours of the night, rather than day, it being her whim to reverse the natural order of things.

Roger Mortimer, Richard Onslow, Peter Willett,
*British Flat Racing,* 1978

*Andrew Devonshire, except in one instance not the luckiest of owners, gives in his book* Park Top *many vivid glimpses of the exhilaration and anxiety that are the common lot of owners. In this passage he conveys some of the more sophisticated fascinations of racing and of the way in which it attracted painters and writers :*

. . . for countless thousands of people racing has a peculiar fascination, of which betting is only one aspect. This fascination is difficult to analyse; obviously, beauty is a strong element, for thoroughbreds are noble, hand-some animals, and the gaudy silks worn by the jockeys enhance their beauty. Then, there is the noise of horses galloping: there is no more thrilling sound than the collective thunder of horses' hooves as they race for the winning post. To all this must be added the excitement of the race itself, with all its hopes and expectations, hopes which are triumphantly fulfilled or cruelly ex-posed as vain aspirations within the twinkling of an eye.

There may be some philistines among those who follow racing, but there are many who are not. Race-horses and racing have attracted painters of the highest calibre ever since the sport first took roots in this country at the end of the seventeenth century. Among the first was the Dutchman Tillemans, who painted scenes of Newmarket Heath in the early part of the eighteenth century – a scene in which today only the garb of the riders and grooms has changed. After Tillemans came a host of others including John Wootton and James Seymour, both of whom painted Flying Childers owned by my ancestor the 2nd Duke of Devonshire. This horse was reputed to be 'the fleetest horse that ever ran at Newmarket, or as is generally believed, that was ever bred in the world'. Next there was Stubbs, although he only painted one picture of an actual race in progress, and that is in the background. This is his famous picture of Eclipse at the Rubbing House at Newmarket. Not long afterwards came Francis Sartorius, Ben Marshall, John Ferneley and John Francis Herring, and after him his son, also John Francis. The Impressionists had their admirers of the racing scene in Degas, Monet and Toulouse-Lautrec, while in more conventional style there were Emil Adam and Lynwood Palmer, and in more recent times Alfred Munnings.

The great nineteenth-century novelists were also aware of the fascination of racing. It comes into Disraeli's novels and plays an important part in the fifth of Trollope's great political series, *The Duke's Children*, while his *The Kellys and the O'Kellys* has the winning of the Derby as one of the main strands in the plot. More recently, Galsworthy brought in many knowledgeable references to racing in his books, and the grandstand at Epsom holds the centre of the background of the view from The Hollies, old Jolyon's house in the Forsyte Saga. On a humbler level there have been many racing novelists from Nat Gould and Edgar Wallace to Dick Francis.

Racing has its place in the arts because of its beauty, glamour and drama. For owners, breeders and trainers it has a further great attraction, for it is a sport in which it is extremely difficult to be successful. For owners and breeders there can be no sure way to success. Certainly, anyone with the money can buy their way into racing, but they cannot be sure they are buying success. Many is the man who has spent a king's ransom on yearlings only to be rewarded with scant success. Luck is an essential element. One leading French trainer is reputed to enquire if approached by an owner to take his horses, not whether the man can be relied upon to pay his training bills or whether he is easy to get on with and to work for, but 'is he lucky?' Only those who are involved in racing know just how difficult it is to win a race of even the most modest kind. For those who love racing it is the extreme competitiveness of the sport which makes winning a race, any race, the most exciting thing in the world.

Andrew Devonshire, *Park Top*, 1976

*The purchasing and racing career of Park Top illustrate, par excellence, the importance of luck. Bought for a song, and more than once nearly sold in the earlier stages of her career, Park Top ended her days conceivably the best English-bred race mare of this century. 'The best of her sex I've ever ridden,' Lester Piggott wrote to her owner after winning the King George VI and Queen Elizabeth Stakes at Ascot in 1969. In all, Park Top won £137,000 in prize money and her races included the Ribblesdale, the Coronation Cup, and the Hardwicke Stakes, as well as narrow defeats in the Prix de l'Arc de Triomphe and the Eclipse, both arguably due to errors of jockeyship.*

[43]

*Lord Rosebery, hard-hitting county cricketer who gave Jack Hobbs his 'cap', Liberal MP and Turf big-wig, owner, breeder, and elder statesman until his death in 1974 at the age of 92, was not everyone's cup of tea. But he had a true passion for racing and the money and determination to satisfy it. He won the Derby, the Oaks, and the St Leger. Kenneth Young describes one of his more engaging aspects, the trouble he took over the felicitous naming of his racehorses:*

Rosebery never had any inhibitions about the fact that he was half Jewish. To a would-be buyer of one of his fillies who protested at the price asked, he remarked with a hearty chuckle, 'You don't expect to get a bargain from me, do you? After all, look at my pedigree – by a Scottish sire from a Jewish dam!' . . .

One of his horses – which won at the Ayr Western meeting in 1961 – was called Allenby, after the general whom he served and deeply admired during the First World War. It was by Never Say Die out of Camp Fire. Even better was his dubbing of the offspring of Bellicose out of Exhibitionist: he called it Monty after the Field Marshal.

In 1963 he named a bay colt yearling Caruso – by Sing Sing out of Donna. His filly Alcohol was by Alcide out of Temptress. He chuckled, too, over Bun Fight out of Must Eat by Combat, and Password by We Don't Know out of Setback. One of his best efforts was Jolly Roger out of Blue Peter and Saucy Wench; another was Adolescence, parents being Never Say Die and Never Say No.

Curiously enough Rosebery's father, the 5th Earl, enjoyed the same sort of fun in naming his horses. One he christened The Bastard. There was much tut-tutting, to which Rosebery replied that no one seemed to know their Shakespeare. When the horse was sold to an Australian owner, the prim antipodeans renamed it The Buzzard.

Presumably neither the 5th nor the 6th Earl had read Henry Kingsley's novel, *Ravenshoe* (1861), in which he protested against the absurdity of the naming of some race horses, giving as examples Allow Me, Ask Mamma and a Derby runner called Suryakumari. In the early 1860s, Professor George Saintsbury tells us, there was a horse called Baktchiserai. With this name, racing people had, however, little trouble; she simply became Back-Kitchen Sarah.

Kenneth Young, *Harry, Lord Rosebery*, 1974

# Trainers

> The sight of a string of thoroughbreds winding slowly home through a village street on a summer morning is one of the pleasantest sights in English country life.
>
> John Hislop, *The Turf,* 1948

At the beginning of the nineteenth century many trainers were nothing more than training grooms, low-paid servants with few social graces. How would these 'breeches and gaiters' men, living the simple life in 'remote corners of the downs and wolds' have regarded the leading trainers of the late nineteenth century to whom, in the words of the Earl of Suffolk, in his *Racing and Steeplechasing* (1886), 'it was quite the ordinary thing to be tall-hatted, frock-coated, kid-gloved and patent-leather-booted' and who dwelt in 'handsome and comfortable residences . . . with fine gardens, trim lawns for croquet and lawn-tennis, billiard rooms, and cellars containing choice vintages'?

Wray Vamplew, *The Turf: a social and economic history of horse-racing,* 1976

*There are trainers today in all categories: from those for whom half a dozen winners constitutes a good season, to those who expect, year in, year out, to train anything between thirty and a hundred winners. In 1975 Peter Walwyn, leading trainer for the second successive year, won 120 races, worth £373,563. The following year Henry Cecil, at the age of 33, was leading trainer, with prize money of £261,041 from 61 races. Between 1900 and 1960 only C. F. N. Murless earned in one season more than £100,000 in prize money, and he did it three times,* in 1957, 1959 and 1960. Since 1965 every leading trainer has won more than £100,000 in prize money. Yet, among over four hundred licensed trainers, the winners of less than one in five reached even double figures in 1975, a ratio that has been constant over the last decade.

In 1830 the weekly training charges were in the region of £1.15s. per horse. In 1920 it was £5. Today it varies between £50 and £120, depending on how fashionable the trainer. These are basic charges. To keep a horse in training in 1981 it costs an average of £5,000 a year, which figure includes entry fees, travelling expenses, and jockey fees.

The more celebrated trainers today can expect to have over a hundred horses in their care; at the other end of the scale many have less than twenty, a figure below which the business is rarely viable. Some trainers gamble to make ends meet, many do not. Disappointed owners often sack them, others fail to pay their bills. The Duchess of Montrose, known as 'Old Six Mile Bottom' and who changed trainers more than most, dismissed one with the words, 'Ah Mr Peace – the Peace which passeth all understanding'. Lord Stamford was taken to Court by Joseph Dawson before he could be induced to pay up. William Day declared that some owners paid 'yearly, some in a number of years and some not at all'. John Porter, one of the greatest trainers, remarked that the greatest burden of trainers was not the vulnerability of horses to injury and illness, nor their modest abilities, but 'the ingratitude of some of your employers, who made a great fuss of you during your success but quit you like rats from a sinking ship when you are out of luck'.

Early methods [of training] were as strange as they were severe. Racehorses were vigorously exercised for three hours at a time, being galloped several times during this period and given drinks of water in between gallops and, as often as not, worked in the evening as well. They were sweated, purged and dieted on horse-bread consisting of beans, wheat and rye, ground up and baked, and fed a day old, and they were heavily clothed with their bellies girt in a swaddling-clothes manner. By the nineteenth century training methods had become reasonable; horses were still exercised at four or five o'clock in the morning and were out for two hours or more, but were galloped less severely, and their feeding and clothing approximated to that of the present time. The tendency, today, is to give horses light work, seldom keep them at exercise for more than an hour and a half, and to vary the routine of exercise.

John Hislop, *The Turf*, 1948

*One of the first to make lasting impact by his elevated style of living as well as by his success was William Chifney (1789–1862), the elder son of Samuel Chifney (1753–1807), the greatest jockey of his time, and elder brother to Samuel Chifney, an even greater jockey than his father.*

*Although only William Chifney of the three belongs properly to the history of training, the family exploits in one form or another dominated the first half of the nine-teenth century. The father has been described thus:*

An exceptionally gifted rider whose hands enabled him to exercise far greater control over horses than most heavier and apparently stronger men. Standing 5 feet 5 inches high, he could go to the scale at 7st. 12 lb. throughout his career. His efforts to be a dandy made him almost effeminate; love locks flowed out from the front of his cap to frame his forehead, and he was much addicted to the wearing of ruffs and frills, while bunches of ribbons adorned the tops of his boots.

Roger Mortimer, Richard Onslow, Peter Willett,
*British Flat Racing*, 1978

In 1791 Chifney was accused of pulling the Prince of Wales's horse Escape to get a better price in a race the following day, which he won. The Prince was advised by the Stewards of the Jockey Club not to employ Chifney again; instead he sold off his horses and retired from the Turf. Chifney retired soon afterwards, having won the Derby in 1789 on Skyscraper and the Oaks four times, in 1789 achieving the Epsom classic double. He is famous, above all, though, for what became known as the 'Chifney rush', saving his horse for a late run in the manner associated with Harry Wragg, the 'head waiter', in the 1930s. Vain and foppish though he may have been, Chifney was the most delicate of jockeys. Pulling up, he wrote in his immodest autobiography Genius Genuine, should be done 'as though you have a silken rein, as fine as a hair, and you were afraid of breaking it'. He invented a bridle with a special bit, which though it later became generally used, he failed at the time to market. He was committed to the Fleet prison for his debt to a saddler and died there aged fifty-three. Brilliant though he was as a jockey, he seems to have been less courageous in the hunt.

Old Chifney – one of the great riding artists of his day on the turf – cut but a poor figure when following the hounds, being excessively timid, a fact well known to his Royal Highness the Prince of Wales, who always ordered him to take the lead over difficult or unknown fences, a post of honour which the jockey dared not, of course, decline. One day, having had a rather severe fall over a fence which the Prince had sent him to explore, the unlucky Chifney shouted to the Prince, 'A ditch, by jingo, your Royal Highness, and I have just about broken my neck over it, don't *you* try, or your neck will soon be done for!'

Ellangowan, *Sporting Anecdotes*, 1889

*Samuel Chifney junior perfected his father's waiting technique, and despite a casual attitude to his profession and an attachment to grand country-house style – he kept tame foxes on his 80-acre stud farm – managed to ride the winner of two Derbys and five Oaks, as well as the 2,000 and 1,000 Guineas. He won the 1,000 Guineas on his last mount, Extempore, at the age of 57.*

The beau ideal of a jockey – elegance of seat, perfection of hand, judgment of pace all united, and power in his saddle beyond any man of his weight who ever sat one. He is averse to making the running, sometimes to a fault. Let whatever number of horses start, Chifney is almost certain to be amongst the last until towards the end of the race, when he creeps up to his brother jockeys in a manner peculiarly his own. But it is in the rush at the finish that he is so pre-eminent.

'Nimrod', *Nimrod Abroad*, 1893

*Between 1810 and 1830, when he won the Derby with his own horse Priam, William Chifney was one of the leading trainers in England, winning the Derby three times and the Oaks twice. He, too, was no stranger to drama, at the age of eighteen serving six months in prison for assaulting the Prince of Wales's stud manager, Colonel Leigh, who had questioned his father's honesty. At the height of his success, when he trained for the Duke of Cleveland and brought off innumerable betting coups, Chifney built for himself Warren House. He died in poverty. John Hislop describes him as 'the severest trainer of his time', who subjected his horses to 'eight-mile sweats and frequent and vigorous gallops', breaking down many in the process.*

*The outstanding trainers in the second half of the nineteenth century were the four Dawson brothers, John Porter of Kingsclere, the Days – John Barham Day and his sons John and William – and Sam Darling. Racing has always run in families and the same names – whether as owners, jockeys or trainers – occur over and over again during the last 150 years. Such names as Scott, Darling, Leach, Piggott, Smyth, Rees, Walwyn come immediately to mind out of many others.*

*Matthew Dawson (1820–98), after John Scott the most important public as opposed to private trainer, trained the winners of twenty-seven classic races, including the St Leger (seven times), the Derby (six times) and the Oaks (five times):*

A short stocky man, with bright, humorous blue eyes, and clean-shaven until old age, he was always immaculately dressed. When he rode out to supervise the work of his string in the morning, he wore a silk top hat, unless he had had more than a sufficiency of the whisky from his native Scotland the previous evening, in which case he favoured a soft felt hat, a signal to the lads that his usually equable temper might be a little ruffled.

Roger Mortimer, Richard Onslow, Peter Willett,<br>
*British Flat Racing*, 1978

*The most influential trainer in the last twenty years of the nineteenth century was John Porter of Kingsclere, who began his career in training at seventeen, when appointed head lad to William Goater at Findon in Sussex (where today Ryan Price, Josh Gifford, and Diane Oughton have their yards).*

*After a period at Cannons Heath, training for Sir Joseph Hawley – a secretive, hypocritical, and unloved man, celebrated mainly for his many and usually unsuccessful battles with Admiral Rous over reforms in racing – Porter moved with his patron to Kingsclere. When Hawley died in 1875 Porter bought the yard and trained there until his retirement. He won the triple crown three times, with the great Ormonde, Common, and Flying Fox; in all he won twenty-three classic races, including seven Derbys and six St Legers. It was Porter who, despite an unsuccessful period of training horses for the Prince of Wales, was enabled by his intervention to found and develop Newbury racecourse:*

Many and many a time, when travelling by rail between Newbury and London, I had cast covetous glances at the level stretch of land immediately to the south of the railway, and within half a mile of Newbury station. It always seemed to me an ideal situation for a racecourse. When I thought of the large number of training stables within a radius of a few miles – those at Lambourn, Wantage, Ilsley, East Wiltshire, and North Hampshire – I convinced myself that the enterprise I had in mind was sure to be a success.

The land I wanted belonged to Mr Lloyd H. Baxendale, of Greenham. Having decided that I would endeavour to convert my ideas into tangible form, I approached the owner, and found him willing to sell. My next step was to have sketch plans and particulars prepared. Armed with these I boldly approached the Jockey Club with a view to securing a provisional licence. They were not as ready to approve my scheme as I had hoped; indeed, they applied to it a liberal douche of cold water. . . .

This interview took place in the Jockey Club Rooms at Newmarket. When I got outside I happened to meet King Edward.

'Hullo! Porter,' he exclaimed, 'what have you been after?'

'I've been trying, your Majesty, to persuade the Stewards of the Jockey Club to grant me a licence for a racecourse at Newbury.'

'And what do they say?'

'They think there are already as many meetings as are required, and they have not yet given a definite answer.'

'Are those the plans you have under your arm?'

'Yes, sir.'

'Then come and see me in the morning, and bring them with you.'

The interest which the King thus manifested in the venture cheered me very much. I duly kept my appointment with his Majesty, explained to him the plans, and expounded the details of the scheme so far as they had been worked out. When I left I felt I had secured a powerful ally.

My next interview with the Jockey Club Stewards was conducted in a very friendly atmosphere, and I got the licence without further trouble.

*John Porter of Kingsclere: an autobiography,* 1919

# Jockeys

No better rider ever crossed a horse;
Honour his guide, he died without remorse.
Jockeys attend – from his example learn
The meed that honest worth is sure to earn.

Epitaph on a celebrated jockey

I have been asked who, in my opinion, was the greatest
jockey of all time. I answer unhesitatingly, Fred Archer,
not because he was England's finest jockey, but because
he is generally admitted to be the best any tracks have
ever known.

Steve Donoghue, quoted in Steve (1974)<br>by Michael Seth-Smith

*'Once a champion, always a champion', seems to hold
truer of jockeys than of almost any other sportsmen. Few
cricketers, for example, however good, head the batting
averages year after year without interruption. Yet the list
of champion jockeys between 1846 and 1979 reveals an
extraordinary consistency. E. Flatman was champion
jockey seven years in succession from 1846–52. G. Fordham was champion from 1855–69, with the exception of
1864 and 1866. Fred Archer was champion from 1874–86.
Between 1891 and 1897 M. Cannon was champion except
for the year 1893. From 1914 onwards the pattern is even
more striking. S. Donaghue was champion ten years in
succession. G. Richards was champion twenty-six times in
twenty-nine years, between 1925 and 1953. D. Smith was
champion five times out of the next six. L. Piggott was
champion eight years in a row between 1964 and 1971. It
is only in the last seven years, when W. Carson, P. Eddery*

(*four times in succession*), *and J. Mercer have alternated as champion that the pattern has showed signs of changing.*

*Top jockeys are certainly the rich men of the Turf, since they make the most money without any capital investment and with few running costs. Wray Vamplew in his book* The Turf: a social and economic history of horse-racing, *quotes an article by J. Runciman in the* Contemporary Review *of 1889:*

The commonest jockey-boy in this company of manni-kins can usually earn more than the average scholar or professional man, and the whole set receive a good deal more of adulation than has been bestowed on any soldier, sailor, explorer, or scientific man of our generation.

*Although Vamplew is concerned mainly with economics (and morality) he discusses sensibly many aspects of racing employment. About retainers to jockeys he observes:*

Retainers rose even more strikingly than presents in the later decades of the nineteenth century. Frank Butler,

Sam Rogers and Jem Robinson, all leading jockeys in the 1830s and 1840s, respectively received £100 from Lord Derby, £50 from Colonel Lowther, and £25 from Mr Ross. Contrast these with George Fordham's perennial £1,000 from Mr Stirling Crawfurd, Archer's £3,600 in 1881, Tod Sloan's £5,000 from Lord William Beresford in 1899, and £15,000 given to Tom Cannon for a three-year retainer in the 1880s. Many of the top jockeys later in the century obtained substantial retainers for third or even fourth call on their services. Unlike presents which were paid after success, retainers were an attempt, sometimes a costly one, to ensure that success. The rising cost of retainers reflected the intensifying struggle to secure the services of top-rank jockeys; and, of course, to keep them off someone else's horses.

*Some great jockeys have lived ascetically, early to bed and early to rise, starving themselves; others have kept appetite at bay with a diet of champagne and cigars. Still others, like Michael Beary and Steve Donoghue, loved the bright lights and lived life to the full. About Donoghue 'the most fascinating character among the jockeys of the past fifty years', Quintin Gilbey wrote :*

For many years his name was associated with that of a lady of title, and when that romance ended others took its place. He loved pink champagne (who doesn't?) and enjoyed few things more than to sit at a *chemin-de-fer* table in a casino, with a pile of chips in front of him, his current girlfriend at his elbow and a bottle of what he called 'The Rosie' in an ice bucket within reach. Although they came from very different backgrounds Steve and Aly Khan had many characteristics in common, not least being the charm which turneth away wrath. Steve's ability to charm irate owners, trainers, and sometimes fellow jockeys into sitting down and

accepting his hospitality was matched by Aly's ability
to pacify outraged husbands who had vowed to kill him.

*Champions All,* 1971

*Discussing techniques of race riding in his book* The Turf
*(1948), John Hislop contrasts the adaptability of British
jockeys with the more rigid style of their American and
Australian counterparts.*

The short stirrup leathers and reins and low crouch of
the Americans and Australians present a neatness and
uniformity that are often lacking in the more upright
stance and longer rein and leathers of the British
jockeys, whose style differs considerably with individuals, although the principle remains the same. . . .
With nervous and highly-strung horses the English
style is undoubtedly the better, and horses which, at the
starting gate, would be driven mad by a short hold of
their heads are different animals in the hands of such
as the late Steve Donoghue, the present champion
Gordon Richards, or any first-class exponents of
English methods.

*In 1897 Tod Sloan came to England from America, his
immediate success revolutionizing English tactics, though
these were later adapted to get the best out of both
methods. In Hislop's words Sloan's 'short stirrup leathers
and reins, low crouch and habit of making the running
from start to finish was at first viewed by the racing world
in the same spirit as Victorian society received the theory
of Darwin'. Nevertheless, English jockeys, influenced still
more by the brilliance of another American, Danny Maher,
began to adopt the American seat. It was Donoghue who,
Hislop continues,*

was the perfect example of the American style adapted
to English conditions; his seat had the neatness of the
American pattern, without exaggeration, and he always

rode with the length of rein best suited to English conditions and the comfort and efficiency of his horse, while he combined strength of horsemanship with the gentleness of a true horse-lover, possessing perfect hands, cool judgement and brilliant dash, qualities which placed him in a class on his own.

*The four great jockeys of modern times, household names even to those who have never sat on a horse nor visited a racecourse, are Fred Archer, Steve Donoghue, Gordon Richards, and Lester Piggott. Of these Donoghue was the most articulate, the most able to express what it actually feels like to ride in a race:*

To me the thrilling moment is when you canter down to the barrier and hear the roar of the crowd. It always reminds me of the sea bounding against the shore. It seems to hold not only encouragement but a bit of a threat – the threat of indifference for a jockey who is up on a loser. But at the break my excitement leaves me. I am so completely in the race that I forget the crowds. My horse and I talk together. We don't hear anyone else. Sometimes on the stretch where we've been out in front and finish easing up I have caught the yell, 'Come on Steve!', but during most of my races I hear it only dully – almost not at all. It is then that the cheers of the crowd make me very happy.

Quoted in Michael Seth-Smith, *Steve*, 1974

*Quoted in the same book is a description of Donoghue, taken from a New York paper, on the jockey's arrival in America to ride Belmont:*

He is a pocket edition man. He is small proportioned, with a tiny pair of feet that many a woman would envy. His powerful shoulders and arms – just the kind for a race-rider who is a whirlwind finisher – are his most striking characteristics. He has regular features, black hair, brown eyes and a fetching smile. The tan of galloping horses out in the open is on his cheeks. He wore a grey pin check coat, cut rather loosely and brown pin check trousers, as though his man had got his suits slightly mixed, when he laid them out – a white silk shirt with a soft collar, a blue and white spotted tie and a grey soft hat. He wore slightly worn tan brogues with rather high heels.

*If Donoghue was the jockey the public most took to their heart – for his human qualities as much as for his style and effectiveness – there can be no doubt that over the years the most consistent jockey has been Gordon Richards. 'The most beautiful scene in the world,' Quintin Gilbey wrote in 1937, 'Gordon Richards, leading by two lengths with a hundred yards to go and his whip still swinging, when you have had twice your limit on him and four times as much as you can afford to lose.'*

*About Lester Piggott as the greatest living jockey there has never been argument. 'No feat of jockeyship ever performed by any man, alive or dead, could not have been carried out equally well, and nine cases out of ten a damn side better, by Lester Piggott,' Gilbey, perhaps the best judge of modern jockeys, states without equivocation and continues :*

I read somewhere that he would be an even greater jockey if he let his leathers down a couple of holes . . . I know he has long legs, and if he was going to ride round Aintree, which his grandfather did with such skill, I have no doubt he would ride half a dozen holes longer, but as he is able to maintain perfect control when perched like a pea on a drum, he would be crazy to ride any other way. The advantage of riding so short is that it places all the jockey's weight on the horse's shoulders, and only the saddle, which in Lester's case often weighs scarcely a pound, rests on the horse's back.

*Champions All,* 1971

*There are fine jockeys around today – the dynamic Carson, the stylish Mercer, the composed Eddery, to name only three – but the great quartet in the modern history of the Turf, the immortals, remain Archer, Donoghue, Richards, and Piggott.*

# Breeding

Our English racehorses differ slightly from the horses of every other breed; but they do not owe their difference and superiority to descent from any single pair, but to continued care in selecting and training many individuals during many generations.

Charles Darwin, *On the Origin of Species*, 1859

In the course of my racing career the studs belonging to Lord Derby, M. Boussac and the Aga Khan reached pinnacles of success hitherto undreamed of in the history of the Turf; but although each of them went through these periods when it seemed futile to contest their supremacy, they all declined. So rapid and catastrophic was their fall from grace that in the space of a few short years the produce of families which had reigned supreme were no longer good enough to contest the classics. Success and failure in racing are built on a variety of factors, but I have little doubt there is one common factor contributing to the decline of these three great studs. Hindsight knowledge can make wizards of us all, and it now seems clear that in all three studs speed was neglected to some extent in an endeavour to introduce more stamina.

Quintin Gilbey, *Champions All*, 1971

*Kentucky is one of the great breeding places of the world. After a visit in 1975 to the studs of the 'Blue Grass' country I wrote this:*

For him, who is above preliminaries,
It is no more than the seigneurial
Raising of hooves round a mane,
A brief thrusting. He strolls off
Lordly as the sun, indifferent now
To the mare, her bride's eyes dying.
But for that other, amiable,
Grey around the lip, who never
Quite made it, civilities
Of courtship are what he must settle for –
Eyes hazy with love-light, the nuzzle
Of arched necks, legs quivering
As if caressed by cool breezes. She bridles,
Looses her urine. And removed from her,
Pawing stubble in the distance,
He must comfort himself with a suitor's
Dwindling euphoria, remembering
Her shiver, sweat drying on his skin.

'Stallion and Teaser' from *Death Valley*, 1980

*Geoffrey Holloway's extraordinarily evocative short poem
was written four years later :*

Wind splits the mare's tail
Like palm fronds under its belly.
Its mane challenges –
Something out
Of helmeted Thermopylae.

Four of its legs prod bonily off
Then rush.
It's that tomfool of a foal again,
Trying to straddle her
At right angles.

'Oedipus at Newmarket', 1979

*Hyperion, one of the smallest Derby winners, had four white socks. Until his victory the following lines were accepted as the classic guide :*

> One white foot, ride him for your life.
> Two white feet, give him to your wife.
> Three white feet, give him to your man.
> Four white feet, sell him – if you can!

*Subsequently, another old saying found more favour :*

> One white foot, keep him not a day;
> Two white feet, send him soon away;
> Three white feet, sell him to a friend;
> Four white feet, keep him to the end.

Exactly what proportion of a horse's merit is due to his conformation is impossible to determine; all that can be said with certainty is that although much should rightly be attributed to nervous energy, the rate and power of nerve stimulus and response, courage and temperament, nevertheless, be the amount great or small, conformation must at least have some value, and that this is the very general view is apparent at every sale ring, where there is no doubt whatever make and shape command a price.

P. E. Ricketts, *Flat Racing*, 1940

# All-Rounders

*Probably the three best autobiographies by men actively involved in racing are the Hon. George Lambton's* Men and Horses I Have Known *(1924), Jack Leach's* Sods I Have Cut on the Turf *(1961), and John Hislop's* Far From a Gentleman *(1954), which just about span the first half of this century. Leach himself refers to Lambton's book as the best book on racing he ever read. Lambton was just about everything it was possible to be in racing – a great trainer over many years who won thirteen Classics, including the Derby with Sansovino and Hyperion, jockey, owner, racing manager – and he comes over in his book as exceptionally decent. Nice men rarely write well, but Lambton's prose is full of vivid, observant touches.*

*Perhaps the most memorable passages in a book even richer in racing lore than Leach's two books, and as packed with good stories, are those about Matthew Dawson and Fred Archer. They show not only the stylish ease of Lambton's manner but the unobtrusive way in which expert comment is communicated.*

Lord Falmouth, Mat Dawson and Fred Archer were names to conjure with. The combination of owner, trainer and jockey had been extraordinarily successful. Most of their great triumphs were before I went racing regularly. I only knew Lord Falmouth slightly, but enough to know that he had supreme confidence in his trainer and jockey and turned a deaf ear to the malicious rumours which always attack success.

Matthew Dawson trained at Heath House, Newmarket. He did things on a lavish scale, and the principle of 'Look after the pennies and the pounds will look after themselves' found no favour with him.

In spite of his strong, fearless character, which would brook no interference from any man in what he thought the duties of his profession, he was the most courteous of men both to his employers and to those who worked for him, and I never met anyone in any rank of life who had not the greatest respect for him, while those who knew him well loved him.

But he had no use for weak men or bad horses. He was never a big better, and was continually warning me against the folly of betting beyond one's means, saying that, although he had the good fortune to have trained more good horses than any other man in the world, on the occasions when he had put more money than usual on a horse it had generally been beaten. Apart from this, he had a contempt for money in itself, and used to call Archer, who had an eye to the main chance, 'that d——d long-legged, tin-scraping, young devil'.

His appearance in the morning at exercise would astonish us in these days; a tall hat, varnished boots, and usually a flower in his buttonhole – for he was almost as good a gardener as he was trainer. Like many people of those times his language was strong, but, as it rolled out of his mouth in broad Scotch, it sounded almost like a benediction. . . .

*Lambton's first Classic win was in 1896 and the last in 1933. He was seventy-three years old when he trained Hyperion to win both the Derby and the St Leger for Lord Derby, upon which his employer retired him on account of his age. He immediately started up on his own, and in the next five seasons won the Victoria Cup, the Chester Cup, the Queen's Prize, the Free Handicap and the Irish 1,000 Guineas.*

*Jack Leach's Sods I Have Cut on the Turf is a wonderful mixture of advice and gossip, technical expertise and anecdote. His chapters on jockeys, racehorses, training and betting are models of lucid exposition, in which sound principles are supported by personal experiences. There are chapters, too, on buying horses, coups, and crooked racing, which offer salutary warnings to the unwary. Two of the most typical things, though, which show different aspects of his manner, are his pieces on race riding and on Edgar Wallace, one of Leach's racing cronies, who included in their number Fred Astaire and Jimmy Wilde. Leach was a stylish and strong jockey but soon after riding the winner of the 1927 2,000 Guineas, weight troubles turned him to training. He trained several good horses at Newmarket between 1931 and 1950 without having a classic winner, but it was as a character and a brilliant journalist – mainly for the* Observer *– that he belongs to the history of the Turf.*

    *Here is part of his chapter on race riding :*

The best way I can describe some of the things one must take into account in race riding is to write about the Two Thousand Guineas which I won on Adam's Apple. I can remember practically every stride, even now. There were twenty-three runners, and I was drawn well, number five, in that wide Newmarket racecourse. Before the race I thought that Call Boy, the favourite, would win – he was ridden by Charlie Elliott and drawn somewhere about the middle, with Hot Night, another very much fancied horse ridden by Harry Wragg, next to him.

My horse behaved perfectly at the gate, giving me every chance to concentrate on getting the best of the start. I stood him about half a length behind the horses on either side of me and when I thought it was going to be a 'go' I got a couple of steps into the tapes just as they went up, getting about three-quarters of a length start . . .

When the field settled down in the first hundred yards I glanced across and saw that Call Boy had gone about three-quarters of a length in front, with Hot Night on his hip, and pulling. I remember thinking at the time that Harry Wragg must be cursing because his horse was running much too free in this early stage. I also thought I'd like to be tracking those two, but it was too far to move over and one can't have everything.

My horse had settled down beautifully; in fact it was, as the saying goes, 'doing nothing'. When we went under the seven furlong gate, he pricked his ears, had a good look at the uprights at the side of the course, and eased himself up very slightly. This put me about one and a half lengths behind Call Boy, but I was pleased about this as I was going so easily and Adam's Apple was enjoying himself.

Coming to the six furlong gate he did the same thing and again at the five; it lost him about half a length each time, but was giving him a wonderful breather without me having to move a muscle – he never got unbalanced. By this time Call Boy was about three to four lengths in front of me with Hot Night still on his hip and still pulling. Going up to the Bushes, the landmark at Newmarket just over two furlongs from home, there is a slight rise, and I gave Adam's Apple an easer. This put me about another half a length behind the leaders, but I knew it would be worth its weight in gold in that last uphill furlong.

I had known exactly what Call Boy and Hot Night had been doing right from the start and thought that they were both running too free, racing against each other. Now, when I took this slight easer, Harry Breasley on Damon came alongside me but was getting uneasy; he had just begun 'pushing'. I looked quickly for other dangers, but realized that the two in the middle were the ones I had to beat.

Past the Bushes with no change, and I was still sitting still. Now I should soon make a move, as there is a really good run down the hill into the Dip, starting almost exactly two furlongs from home. I just gave Adam's Apple the office to quicken, and so had him really running half-way down the hill. One must always be nearly on top here as it helps to carry one up the other side. I was still about one and a half lengths behind Call Boy, but making it up fast. Going into the Dip I pulled my whip – when you are coming from behind to challenge you must throw everything in, especially when, as I realized at this moment, it was going to be a very near thing. Adam's Apple responded well, but Call Boy pulled a bit out too – he was a great horse that day, as he was when he won the Derby. The last fifty yards was a tremendous battle – Hot Night had tired half-way up the hill, but then Sickle came with a late run and got nearly to my girths.

All three horses, Adam's Apple, Call Boy, and Sickle ran as straight as gun-barrels and as game as fighting cocks. I was certain I had won, but was glad to see the number twenty-six in the frame because when we were pulling up I heard Charlie Elliott tell one of the other jockeys that he thought he had just lasted home. I think the wish was father to the thought. However, we were running wide of each other and it was only a short head, so naturally he was hoping.

*The following Wallace sketch is preceded by others on race-course characters such as the prizefighter Jimmy Carney ('There shouldn't ever be a last race – they ought to do away with it') and the Pie Kid, a runner for professional backers: 'He knew everybody, what they were doing, and what they were likely to do in future. He also knew where everybody was. I arrived in London one day on leave and wanted to find some of the boys. I saw Pie in Piccadilly and he told me "Harry Wragg is visiting a nursing home in Chester Square, Gordon is lunching at Scotts, and Charlie Elliott is at the Turkish baths".'*

Edgar Wallace was a friend of mine, and what a fantastic man he was. In many ways he was a strong personality, but there was one very weak link in his make up – he thought he knew everything about racing. I never met a man who knew less.

He fought a continuous battle against the bookmaker, and hardly won a round. With the few hairtrunks he kept in training, in the belief that they were racehorses, he hadn't much chance. He was as game as a pebble, and the trouble was he was in love with his horses, and wouldn't hear a word against them. If his trainer, or any of the crack jockeys who rode for him from time to time, told him the horses were no good, they immediately got the sack. Everybody liked Edgar; even the trainers and jockeys he sacked remained firm friends. I rode an animal for him at Ally Pally one day which he told me would win. It finished about eighth of twelve runners and there was not the slightest excuse for it. When I came back he asked, 'What happened?' I told him that nothing had happened – it was a moderate horse (moderate was giving it a lot the best of it). I never rode for him again. . . .

*

Edgar used to write racing articles, with tips, for various newspapers; but what he really knew about his subject was a moot point. Edgar thought he knew it all, and I believe he did tip a winner once, when the office boy had got fed up with all the losers and changed the selection. However, Edgar never lost confidence; he always thought the next one was a certainty. . . .

*

I went to see him one evening at his flat in Portland Place. He was striding up and down the room, chain-smoking through that famous long black holder, writing four books at once plus a racing article. I mean he was talking them into microphones and was certainly getting muddled up. Suddenly he turned to me and said, 'There are too many characters in one of these books; I must get rid of some of them, they worry me.' He then murdered four of them in less than one chapter. It was fantastic to listen to.

*

I met his daughter Pat one day, and someone in the party mentioned a book called *Murder on the Second Floor*. I asked Pat, 'Did your father write that?' She replied, most indignantly, 'Of course not. Daddy would have had a murder on every floor.'

I used to travel with Edgar to some of the London meetings, and he had some curious habits. If we passed a funeral he would take his hat off and say 'Thank God he is going straight.'

Another thing I noticed was that when he had had a horse running, he would jot a few things down in a little notebook. One day my curiosity got the better of me and I asked, 'What the devil do you keep putting down in that book?' He said, 'Well, that horse of mine finished in front of four today. I make a note of those animals, and when I get him in a race where the only other runners are horses that have finished behind him, then we will bet.' Of course he should have been entered in a race for horses that would be better dead, but nobody dare suggest this.

I went to the theatre with Wallace once or twice – his own shows of course. He once had about half a dozen running in London at the same time. I remember being in a box with him watching *The Calendar*, which incidentally was the only good racing play I ever saw. I was very amused when he laughed heartily at all the jokes and led the applause with great enthusiasm, and I am certain he enjoyed the show more than anybody else in the house.

*It is John Hislop, with John Oaksey and Brough Scott, who more than anyone has carried on the Lambton–Leach tradition of riding and writing.* Far From a Gentleman (*1954*), Anything But a Soldier (*1965*), Racing Reflections (*1955*), *and* The Brigadier (*1973*) *are admirable examples of racing and breeding experiences described from the inside. The following passage in* Anything But a Soldier *describes how, recovering from a bad fall at Cheltenham, Hislop set himself the task of learning about breeding racehorses:*

To anyone with his heart in it, there is a beauty or poetry in the driest of subjects, and delving into pedigrees I found that this was so in the study of Thoroughbred breeding. There is a saying on the Turf to the effect that a good horse never has a bad name; and it may be that there is some unknown natural law of art and poetry influencing this and other activities in life. At any rate, every now and then I would come across a pedigree which, read in the tail female line, would not have been out of place in Milton or Virgil. For instance: 'Cyllene, by Bona Vista out of Arcadia, by Isonomy out of Distant Shore, by Hermit out of Land's End' – 'Any more will be half a crown,' the late Bert Rich used to say – or: 'Pretty Polly, by Gallinule out of Admiration, by Saraband out of Gaze, by Thuringian Prince out of Eye Pleaser, by Brown Bread out of Wallflower.' Thus my studies became a delight, rather than a chore, illuminated by the mental pictures which they inspired.

I used to imagine what the horses bearing these names were like – Arcadia gay and friendly, Distant Shore quiet and remote; and I wondered what kind of personalities those who had given them these names possessed.

*Earlier on, in* Far From a Gentleman (*1954*), *Hislop describes how at Wellington he first developed a taste for the literature of racing:*

Academically, the only lasting influence which Wellington left me, apart from that of Mr Talboys, was a liking and fair knowledge of Milton's poetry, the main subject for the English examination of the School Certificate of my year. My reading still reflected my enthusiasm for the turf: the poems of Gordon, Patterson and Ogilvie, the latter illustrated by Lionel Edwards, *Right Royal* by John Masefield – I had the edition illustrated by Cecil Aldin – and those two brilliant short stories of Rudyard Kipling, *The Maltese Cat* and *The Broken Link Handicap*, were among my favourites. By then I had begun to read Galsworthy, a writer to whom I became sympathetically inclined after coming across his racing story in *Captures* – a book which my mother did not greatly approve of my reading – and his account of the 'nobbling' of the two-year-old at Ascot in *The Forsyte Saga*.

*Such a list would make a good basis for any anthology. In Hislop's own graceful writings there is a memorable passage about his thoughts on leaving Newmarket, where he had worked as assistant to Victor Gilpin.*

The High Street is still recognizable in old prints of the town when it was no more than a village; and the ageless expanse of the Heath sweeps the wind through the past: Chifney the elder tutoring his little boy, destined to become an even greater jockey than his father, in the art of race riding, on Warren Hill; Charles II, one of the finest amateur riders of his day, winning a race across the Flat; James II, whose heart was in hunting rather than racing, following his hawks across South Fields; Boadicea leading her chariots out of Exning against the Romans.

*John Hislop was leading amateur on the Flat in 1938 and 1939 and again from 1946–55. He also rode many winners over the jumps and was third in the Grand National. All the same, he would probably settle for being remembered, above all, for his exploits with Brigadier Gerard, bred and owned by him, and one of the great racehorses of this century. His book* The Brigadier *(1973) contains fine descriptions of the preparation and racing of a Classic horse. One of the most affecting passages of all, though, comes at the end, before the Brigadier's last race,*

[73]

*the Champion Stakes of 1972. They decided to give him his final gallop on Newbury Racecourse :*

When the morning of the Brigadier's gallop at Newbury dawned there was a fairly dense fog; so much so, that I wondered whether we should be able to work the horses at all. However, it cleared just sufficiently for the purpose, though it would have been too foggy to race.

The Brigadier and Almagest were going seven furlongs the reverse way of the course, that is to say right handed, finishing at the Greenham end of the back straight. The going was beautiful, a real credit to Frank Osgood, who always has the Newbury course in such good order. While the Brigadier knew exactly where he was, he had always galloped and raced up the straight, as the races are run, so was interested to find himself undergoing a different routine. He also realized that he was working towards his horse box and was alert and eager.

Fog sometimes has a disturbing effect on horses, perhaps because they can lose their sense of direction in it, causing them to want to go faster, possibly in the hope of getting out of the fog as soon as possible; and I remember the now-successful trainer 'Fiddler' Goodwill, when he was working for the late Tom Leader, making about six circuits of the Links at Newmarket after the rest of us in the gallop had pulled up, before he succeeded in stopping the mare he was riding.

Happily no such misadventure befell the Brigadier, but he certainly worked with great zest.

There was a dramatic quality about the scene as we stood peering through the Cimmerian gauze, waiting for the horses to emerge. Nothing could be seen of the stands across the course, the silence was complete; we might have been in outer space. Then, faintly at first and gradually increasing, came that unmistakable and thrilling sound, which in two thousand years no writer has succeeded in describing better than Virgil with his, 'quadripedante putrem sonitu quatit ungula campum' – the hoofbeats of galloping horses – and out of the fog burst the Brigadier as he swept past Almagest. At a few yards' distance from him at which I was standing as he passed, he was a magnificent and awe-inspiring sight, ears pricked, nostrils distended, his great, powerful frame and limbs moving with the rhythm and force of an express train, his hooves tearing the turf from under him – my heart bled for Frank's groundsmen – the momentum of his progress leaving the swishing of its slip-stream behind him. His sense of direction beamed on the end of the back straight, where his horse box awaited him, and determined to get there as fast as possible, he was really travelling. In a flash he had vanished into the fog, his hooves beating out in diminuendo until, once again, there was silence.

Never had I seen him work more impressively and in this form I was convinced that no horse in the world was capable of beating him.

With a good heart we faced the Brigadier's last battle, his second Champion Stakes. It was just a matter of all keeping well with him and the weather being kind to us. In both respects fortune favoured us: the Brigadier remained in perfect order and the fine weather held.

*Oaksey, though no collection of his writings exists, belongs in the company of Hislop, for he was in his day an engaging and brave rider over fences who got horses to go for him. As a racing journalist and TV commentator he combines forthrightness with modesty and charm.*

*The following passage comes from his admirable and affectionate* The Story of Mill Reef (*1974*) :

Late at night 19 August, 1970, Ian Balding, who normally sleeps like a hibernating bear, was anxiously pacing the floor of his bedroom a few miles outside York. Since early evening, the rain had been streaming down and in an hotel not far away, it was keeping Geoff Lewis awake too – by splashing into the river outside his window. The same gloomy thoughts were in both their minds – for York racecourse is not called the Knavesmire for nothing and the last thing Mill Reef needed at that stage of his career was another hard race in heavy ground. . . . Geoff Lewis's impression at Maisons-Laffitte had been that Mill Reef could not get a proper grip on the heavily-watered ground and although the little horse had not left a single oat uneaten since that race, it still seemed entirely possible that the experience might have left a lasting mark.

Walking down the stand side of the six furlong course on the morning of the Gimcrack, Ian Balding's worst fears were justified. Deep hoof-prints from the previous day's racing were rapidly filling with water and by the time he arrived at the start, Ian had made up his mind that to run in such conditions would be not only foolish but downright dangerous. At that point, however, he met the assistant starter and was told that the stewards had already decided to place the starting stalls for the straight races on the far side of the course. Walking back along that rail, he found a definite improvement, but the ground was still far softer than anything Mill Reef had ever galloped, let alone raced on.

Left to himself at this stage, Ian would almost certainly have withdrawn there and then, but now for the first time Mr Mellon had come from America to see Mill Reef run. Having gloomily reported the situation to his owner in the Halifax box, Ian suggested that they should at least wait until Geoff Lewis had ridden in the first race of the day.

So around 2.15 that afternoon, less than an hour before declaration time for the Gimcrack, the three men

met in the glass-fronted weighing room at York. Geoff's verdict was emphatic.

'I've never ridden on softer ground in all my life,' he said, and added that if, despite everything, they did decide to run, he would like permission, whatever happened, not to use his whip.

Mr Mellon turned to Ian.

'What would you do if I weren't here?'

'I'm afraid I'd certainly withdraw.'

There was a pause after that and then Mr Mellon said quietly, 'Well, I just have a feeling everything will be all right and that we should run.' He readily gave Geoff the permission he had asked for and assured Ian that the decision had nothing to do with his own presence at York, with the Gimcrack Club or with anything else apart from the horse's welfare.

'I just have this feeling,' he repeated; 'Everything will be all right.'

*

Geoff Lewis's recipe for riding in heavy ground is that once a horse has settled to his stride, you should

[77]

never take him out of it. Accordingly, he let Mill Reef choose his own pace and four horses, Trem Blay, King's Company, Most Secret, and Green God, were a length or so in front of him until half way. There Geoff took stock of the position.

'Frankie [Durr] was riding the ears off Green God,' he says. 'All the others I could see were dead meat – and here am I, just barely going half speed. There didn't seem much point in giving them a second chance, so I let him run for half a furlong. And when I looked round – well, it was unbelievable.'

It was indeed, for in that half furlong, without coming off the bit, Mill Reef had gone four or five lengths clear. Long before the end, Geoff started pulling up – or meant to anyway – but at the line the verdict was still ten lengths. And later, when Ian Balding said jokingly to the judge, John Hancock, 'That didn't test your eyesight too severely,' John replied that, oddly enough, it had been a very difficult distance to assess: 'Because even at the post, your fellow was still going so much faster than the others that, in another hundred yards, he'd have won by twenty lengths, not ten.'

*

It was long after the Gimcrack in fact that Ian Balding found at least a partial answer to the question of how a horse with Mill Reef's flawless, feather-light action could contrive not to be thrown out of gear by the sort of quagmire he encountered at York.

On the morning before the 1971 Prix de l'Arc de Triomphe, Mill Reef and his travelling companion Aldie did a four-and-a-half furlong pipe-opener up a strip of watered gallop near their stables at Lamorlaye. The going was mostly good, except for two or three soft patches. Walking down the gallop afterwards, Ian could see quite clearly where Aldie's hooves had printed the turf, but of Mill Reef's passage there was no sign until he reached the first soft patch. And there the difference was even more glaringly apparent. For while Aldie, a firm ground specialist with a low sweeping action, had cut in three or four inches deep and actually turned the turf over, Mill Reef's small feet had only barely left a mark.

Since that day, his fascinated trainer noticed the same phenomenon many times and so did Jona Holley, the man who lovingly cares for the gallops at Kingsclere.

'It's as though a ghost had galloped by,' says Ian and although neither he nor I had ever heard of such a thing before, there does not seem to be much doubt that some quality in Mill Reef's action enabled him to float where others sank and fly where they could only flounder.

Probably, like most exceptional athletes, his excellence in this respect depended more on timing than strength. And it would be no easier to analyse his action at full stretch than Gary Sobers's on-drive, Barry John's sidestep or the backhand of Ken Rosewall. All you can say for certain is that these were things of beauty – and that their results are on the scoreboard.

# Steeplechasing

*A century ago not everyone took the same delight in steeplechasing as, in general, they do today.*

Portugal has her *auto-da-fé*; dignified Catalonia the *delicate* bullfight; and Rome – elegant, classical, imperial Rome – once gloried in the fights of the gladiators, whose dying agonies were witnessed by her *sensitive* daughters with as much sang-froid as an 'exquisite' of our time watches the pirouette of a fiquarantee. We have our steeple chases, where gentlemen meet in friendly contest to prove the nerve and spirit of an Englishman, and on which bright eyes may look without fear or pain! Let us then be thankful that we live in a country where no *barbarous amusement* is known; and let Englishmen, whose high-mettled steeds never flinch from a rasper – whose courage none ever yet dared doubt – throw up their castors and cry with one accord, 'Long life to Steeple Chasing'.

There could not be a better argument in favour of the abolition of the sport, than the fact of its being placed by its own advocates in the same category with the disgusting, inhuman, and demoralizing bull and gladiator fights.

As to its being 'a manly' sport, is it manly to force into the painful contest the unwilling and helpless animal, or to goad and lash the willing one, when it can go no faster nor farther – plunging the spurs into its panting sides, and raising with the whip weals and sounds at once painful and unsightly, until the blood flows, and exhaustion, if not death, follows? Is it manly to add artificial, dead, and heavy weights to the already overloaded horse; and, when in that state, to furiously ride and urge on the tottering beast to the pointed stake, or throw him on the thick-set edge of thorn and stake; leave him in the ditch or brook, the water or the mud, to writhe with pain, be exhausted from bleeding, and helpless and dying; – the consequence of fractured limbs and severe injuries? . . .

The animal's premeditated and early death would be far preferable, and less cruel than its present wanton and prolonged suffering; and in this light we could look somewhat charitably upon that man who, at one blow on the horse's head, felled the poor dumb creature 'like a bullock' to the ground. Yet the race is continued whether the horses are tired, exhausted, bleeding, lame, or dying, and the lash and spur are applied with re-doubled force to their reeking and quivering sides. In the teeth of this enormity, however, we are unblushingly told that 'we live in a country where no barbarous amusement is known!'

John Harrison, *An Essay on the Evils of Steeple Chasing*, 1851

*Since Harrison's essay there have been few complaints about steeplechasing, despite numerous accidents to both horses and riders. The same is scarcely the case with the Grand National, against which violent outcries have been made at frequent intervals since its first official running, under its present title, in 1847.*

*About steeplechasing Colonel the Hon. E. H. Wyndham wrote in his Foreword to* The History of Steeplechasing *(1966):*

I do not believe that any man, however good a horseman he may be, would be capable of getting a horse round a steeplechase if the animal really disliked the job and was determined not to help in carrying it out.

*The most famous obstacle in the National course is Becher's Brook, named after Captain Becher:*

Becher was on Conrad, and went first to get him to settle down, up to what was then a fence with double rails, and a large ditch dammed up on the far side. The horse made a mistake and hit the rails, and in a second, the gallant captain had 'formed to receive cavalry' by crouching under the bank. As for his charger, he got back on the wrong side, and he lost him, and the place, though sadly degenerated, is called Becher's Brook to this day.

The Druid, *Scott and Sebright*, 1862

Becher was equally as brilliant a performer in the evenings at social gatherings as he was throughout the day in the saddle, his favourite tricks being to run around a room on the wainscoting without touching the floor, kicking the ceiling, and most amazing of all, imitating the noises of almost every known animal.

Michael Seth-Smith in *The History of Steeplechasing*, 1966

*After a successful career Becher – a veteran of the Peninsular War, who served with Wellington in Belgium*

*– ended his days as Inspector of Sacks for the Great Northern Railway at Boston in Lincolnshire.*

*Becher, the dandified Jem Mason, and the Sussex-born Tom Oliver were the great professional steeplechase jockeys of the mid-nineteenth century. After them the amateurs dominated the scene, some of them highly effective, others less so.*

We know of no more humiliating sight than misshapen gentlemen playing at jockeys. . . . What a farce to see the great hulking fellows go to scale with their saddles strapped to their backs, as if to illustrate the impossibility of putting a round of beef upon a pudding-plate.

R. S. Surtees, *Mr Sponge's Sporting Tour,* 1853

'*For the comedy of errors in crossing a country, amateur steeplechases are worth watching,' Druid wrote in* Post and Paddock *in 1856. Roger Longrigg observes, 'The riders were either overdone or underdone, never just right : just right, according to Druid, was "three parts of a bottle of port wine, two glasses of brandy-and-water, and a pipe".'*

*The greatest of the amateurs between 1870 and 1914 was Arthur Yates, who rode 460 winners and trained 2,950 winners. During this golden age of the amateur rider twelve Grand Nationals were won out of fifteen between 1871 and 1885 by amateurs. About Yates Michael Seth-Smith quotes the following verse from* The Sporting Life *after Yates had fallen in a race at Croydon, but catching his horse by the tail as it ran off had re-mounted to win :*

In racing reports it is oftentimes said
That a jockey has cleverly won by a head;
But Yates has performed, when all other arts fail,
A more wonderful feat – for he won by a tail.

[83]

*According to Roger Longrigg, National Hunt racing, when it started again in 1919, 'was still a poor relation, dominated by sportsmen rather than racing men, and infested with crooks'.*

*That is not now the case, and the last thirty years have seen great increases in prize-money, prestige and all-round skill. Successful jumpers are no longer failed flat horses, but a unique breed of their own. The greatest names (quite apart from Grand National winners such as the triple-winning Red Rum and the dual winner Reynoldstown) are as well known for their exploits to the man in the street as the winners of the Derby – such legendary Cheltenham Gold Cup winners as Mandarin, Mill House, Arkle (who won it three times) and L'Escargot, such Champion Hurdlers as Sir Ken, Persian War, Bula, and Comedy of Errors. The great jump trainers of the modern era, Fulke Walwyn, Ryan Price, Fred Rimell, Fred Winter, the great jockeys over fences such as Molony, Mellor, Winter, Gifford, Biddlecombe, Thorner, Davies, and Barry, may not make as much money as their flat race counterparts, but they grace the Turf equally, and, through television, have become household names.*

*If the Derby is the most famous flat race in the world, the Grand National is certainly the greatest steeplechase. People who have only two bets a year have them on these two races. They could scarcely be more different in the nature of their contest, the appearance and breeding of the horses (and of the jockeys for that matter), the texture of the racecourse; summer-silken and green-leaved Epsom, wintry Aintree. John Welcome, racing novelist as well as biographer of the Turf, has written an impressively long novel about it, called simply,* Grand National. *Dick Francis rode in perhaps the most sensational Grand National of all and in the following piece – unpublished in England – he describes what the race has meant to him*

*over the years. It seems the best way to represent the*
*writer whose fifteen or so novels have given to the literature*
*of racing a unique authenticity and excitement :*

When I was seven I saw the road to Paradise as thirty huge fences on four and a half miles of green turf, with heavenly hazards on the way called Becher's, Canal Turn, Valentine's, The Chair. That year, 1928, was when I understood properly what the Grand National Steeplechase was all about.

Two horses only, of a field of 42 starters, reached the last of the fearsome obstacles without falling. An American horse, Billy Barton, was in front, with a hopeless British outsider, Tipperary Tim, on his heels. Billy Barton crashed to the ground as he landed. Tipperary Tim, at 100–1, ridden by an amateur, swept alone along the half-mile stretch to the winning post. The professional rider of Billy Barton, who had broken his collar-bone, remounted and finished second.

I learned that year that the greatest steeplechase in the world could be won by luck, by a moderate horse from a small stable, and by a jockey out there risking his neck for love of the game, not for money. I also learned that the professional view was to pick up the broken pieces and get on with the matter in hand; and I reckon that all that wasn't too bad for seven.

*

In 1956 I nearly won on Devon Loch, who belonged to Queen Elizabeth, the Queen Mother. Nearly, but for about the last forty yards; at which point, frightened I think by the riotous reception from a quarter of a million screaming throats, he suddenly lost his stride and collapsed on to his belly. We had been within spitting distance of winning by ten lengths in a record time, but although he staggered back to his feet he had pulled several muscles, and we never actually completed the course.

The following season I rode him in four more races – two wins, two seconds – but by the next Grand National we were both out of the game from injury. I stood in the Press box instead, and *wrote* about the next winner, Sundew.

*In 1936, twenty years before Francis's sad experience in the National, Anthony Mildmay, 'the last of the Corinthians', suffered an equal disappointment on the 100–1 outsider Davy Jones. The race is described in* The History of Steeplechasing :

Davy Jones was really little more than a novice when he ran in the National. He was a horse that always took a really strong hold and it was Mildmay's custom to tie a knot in the reins when riding him. Just as Davy Jones was leaving the Paddock at Aintree for the parade, Peter Cazalet . . . noticed that Mildmay had not tied his usual knot. He was about to advise him to do so when he changed his mind, thinking that Mildmay had decided not to tie a knot in order to make it easier to slip the reins when landing over the drop fences. This perfectly reasonable decision was to cost Davy Jones the race.

Right from the very first jump, where Golden Miller fell, Davy Jones pulled his way to the front and throughout the first circuit he led the field, measuring fence after fence with faultless accuracy . . . However, Reynoldstown, ridden by Fulke Walwyn, was making up ground and by Becher's had almost drawn level. On they went together, Davy Jones, barely a length to the good, both horses jumping magnificently for their amateur riders. . . .

*Three out Reynoldstown made a mistake. Walwyn lost an iron and it seemed that Davy Jones, with 23 lb. in hand, was certain to win. Mildmay had not moved on him, while Walwyn was hard at work driving Reynoldstown back into the race. Roger Mortimer, in his biography of Anthony Mildmay, takes up the story :*

Davy Jones did not take the second last fence quite cleanly and pecked a little on landing. To give him every chance to recover Anthony let slip his reins to the very buckle, and then in one nightmare moment, disaster descended. The prong of the buckle in some way managed to slip through the hasp, and in a trice, there were the reins flapping loose round Davy Jones's neck. Desperately Anthony tried to guide him with his whip to the final fence. It was of no avail. Davy Jones ran out to the left, and the gallant Reynoldstown was left to win as he pleased from Ego, ridden by Mr Harry Llewellyn, a far less famous figure then than he is today. In a few terrible, unforgettable seconds, the vision that must have seemed to Anthony too good to be true had been cruelly erased.

*Anthony Mildmay, 1955*

*One of the great riders over fences in his day was Roddy Owen, a distinguished and unusually cultivated soldier who served in India, Uganda, and Egypt and died in 1896*

*of cholera at the age of forty. He rode the winner of the*
*Grand National in 1892.*

It is said that a discussion once arose at dinner on the
differences between a cavalry and cross-country seat, a
distinguished officer contending that any good cross-
country rider could at once settle into a cavalry seat
and find no difficulty in doing so. The officer finally
said, 'Let us refer to Roddy. He knows. What do you
say about it?' 'Well, sir,' replied Roddy, who had kept
silent during the discussion, 'the fact is, I am so often
found fault with, sir, that it is rather a sore point with
me. Only the other day on parade, my horse didn't
seem to like my seat and bolted with me. He took me
right down towards the railway station, sir.' Then, after
a pause, he added with the greatest innocence, 'Fortunately he just stopped there in time for me to catch the
2 train to Sandown, where I was due to ride a race
at 3.15.'

From Mai Bovill and G. R. Askwith, *Roddy Owen*, 1897

*Ernest Hemingway was a frequent visitor to French race-*
*tracks. Steeplechasing plays a less important part in*
*French racing than it does in England, but the prize money*
*these days is high and there are good pickings to be had,*
*for owners as well as punters. The following, describing a*
*day at Enghien in the 1920s, comes from* A Moveable
Feast *(1964):*

I decided to go down and buy a morning racing paper.
. . . They were running at Enghien, the small, pretty
and larcenous track that was the home of the outsider.
. . . 'I think we ought to go,' my wife said. 'We haven't
been for such a long time. We'll take a lunch and some
wine. I'll make good sandwiches.'

\*

So we went out by the train from the Gare du Nord

through the dirtiest and saddest part of town and walked from the siding to the oasis of the track. It was early and we sat on my raincoat on the fresh-cropped grass bank and had our lunch and drank from the wine bottle and looked at the old grandstand, the brown wooden betting booths, the green of the track, the darker green of the hurdles, and the brown shine of the water jumps and the whitewashed stone walls and white posts and rails, the paddock under the new-leafed trees and the first horses being walked to the paddock. We drank more wine and studied the form in the paper and my wife lay down on the raincoat to sleep with the sun on her face. I went over and found someone I knew from the old days at San Siro in Milan. He gave me two horses.

'Mind, they're no investment. But don't let the price put you off.'

We won the first with half of the money that we had to spend and he paid twelve to one, jumping beautifully, taking command on the far side of the course and coming in four lengths ahead. We saved half of the money and put it away and bet the other half on the second horse who broke ahead, led all the way over the hurdles and on the flat just lasted to the finish line with the favourite gaining on him with every jump and the two whips flailing.

We went to have a glass of champagne at the bar under the stand and wait for the prices to go up.

'My, but racing is very hard on people,' my wife said. 'Did you see that horse come up on him?'

'I can still feel it inside me.'

'What will he pay?'

'The *cote* was eighteen to one. But they may have bet him at the last.'

The horses came by, ours wet, with his nostrils working wide to breathe, the jockey patting him.

'Poor him,' my wife said. 'We just bet.'

We watched them go on by and had another glass of champagne and then the winning price came up: 85. That meant he paid eighty-five francs for ten.

'They must have put a lot of money on at the end,' I said.

But we had made plenty of money, big money for us, and now we had spring and money too. I thought that was all we needed. A day like that one, if you split the winnings one quarter for each to spend, left a half for racing capital. I kept the racing capital secret and apart from all other capital.

# Some Racecourses

Then peers grew proud in horsemanship t'excell,
Newmarket's glory rose, as Britain's fell.

Alexander Pope

*I watched my first race as a boy in Calcutta in the mid-1930s. In consequence, no course quite compares for me in beauty with Calcutta racecourse, sweeping between the Victoria Memorial and the Hooghly, flags flying from its turrets. Indian racecourses with their flutter of pink, turquoise, and gold saris, the crisp elegance of the men, are unique. W. G. C. Frith has recently written the history of the Club, which was formed in 1847. Until things were put on a more orthodox footing, racing in Calcutta seems to have been both eccentric and strenuous. Frith writes:*

Reading through these early prospectuses [of the 1820s and 1830s] and racing returns, no one can fail to be struck by the apparent severity of the conditions, two and three mile races, three, four and even five heats, horses being described as 'coming under whip and spur', being called upon to race every day there was racing irrespective of fitness or soundness. One account describes a horse as 'having something wrong with him as he was dead lame when he started for the second heat'. Pretty desperate measures were adopted during a race. A Yorkshire jockey who arrived in Poona in 1828 after a hair-raising journey, described how he was persuaded to ride in a big match the day after his arrival. Having won the first heat after a pretty hard race, he was surprised to see his master put the horse's fore legs into a tub of saltpetre and cold water while he drenched it with a pint of warm bear (*sic*) with a nutmeg in it. Strange training methods, but apparently effective as the horse won the second heat all right half an hour later.

*The Royal Calcutta Turf Club,* 1976

*'Bear' presumably is a misprint for beer, but in Calcutta one cannot be too sure. Frith records some unusual races, such as the Cheroot Stakes for untrained Arabs – Gentleman Riders. 'Each to start with a lighted cheroot in his mouth and to keep same alight during the race and to bring it alight to the weighing place or to be considered distanced.' There were seventeen runners and only one cheroot went out. Things were more orderly in my day, though on Monsoon Cup Day, 1930, there took place what came to be known as the 'Tote Robbery'. The tins containing the money from the Saturday's racing were found, when they were taken down to the bank under armed guard on the Monday morning, to contain brick rubble. The mystery was never solved.*

*Although conceding that 'Goodwood is easily the most beautiful racecourse in the world, and no flamingoes, coconut trees, lilies or goldfish are needed to make it so', Jack Leach was at heart a Newmarket man :*

Newmarket is one of the only places where a man can go racing; elsewhere he merely goes to the races, which isn't the same thing at all. At Newmarket the mornings are almost as much a part of the show as the afternoons, and a visitor doesn't have to know anybody or own a badge to get a fair idea of the entire show.

The heath is open so that anybody can stroll across to within a few yards of where the horses are galloping, and as long as he doesn't get too close, and actually in the way, nobody will interfere. If he wants any in-

formation about horses, the touts and newspaper re-
porters are invariably friendly and helpful and will tell
him where to stand to get the best view. On top of this
they will tell him the names of all the horses within a
couple of miles, even if they don't know them.

The visitor to Newmarket will be well advised to get
up very early in the morning, although he may feel that
it hasn't been long enough since last night. It's worth
doing once. He will remember it for a long time, and
it will save having to do it again.

I have ridden work on the downs at Lambourn,
Danebury, Chattis Hill, Epsom and various other
places including the moors at Middleham and the
wolds at Malton. I have also seen the gallops at Beck-
hampton and Druids Lodge on Salisbury Plain, but in
my opinion you can't name the odds on Newmarket for
training racehorses. There is an infinite variety of
gallops; every morning a trainer can select where to
work out of at least ten different places. There are
winter gallops, spring gallops, and in the summer,

during the longest droughts ever known, the Limekilns on the Bury St Edmunds side of the town has never been known to get firm.

\*

Newmarket has had its critics ever since Charles II and his courtiers were hawking over the heath, but it is mostly shelled at long range and any man who has trained there for any length of time rarely leaves to go anywhere else. In 1863 criticism of Newmarket reached such proportions that the owners of all the Derby candidates took them elsewhere to finish their preparations – that is, all except one, Macaroni. Luckily for Newmarket, he won. When Macaroni and his trainer arrived home from Epsom, they were met by the Town Band and the bells were rung at All Saints Church.

From *Sods I Have Cut on the Turf*, 1961

*Although, both for variety and landscape, I prefer English racecourses to all others (and of these Newbury, Lingfield, Fontwell, Sandown, Goodwood, and Plumpton), I do not share Jack Leach's distaste for American tracks. They are usually less part of the countryside than English courses, but many of them have a romantic, sub-tropical beauty, like New Orleans, or Santa Anita, or Gulfstream in Florida :*

RACEHORSES AT GULFSTREAM

Turning for home, at last off the bridle,
They seem as they lengthen their strides

Almost to falter. Beneath them, green thickens,
Goes drowsy, as though a film

Were being slowed, the frame frozen.
They have for a second the air

Of somnambulists, moving loosely
In envelopes of water. An uphill element

Is against them. They break free,
And their actions, recovering, turn languorous,

Muscles slithering in quarters
Transparent under sweat, their veins swollen.

Palmettos and flags become fixed blurs
And towing in their slipstreams long shadows

They dent distance as it dwindles,
Air, earth conniving, their eyes limitless.

Alan Ross, from *Death Valley*, 1980

*Elizabeth Hardwick, the celebrated writer wife of the American poet Robert Lowell, published recently, in 1979, a semi-autobiographical novel* Sleepless Nights. *In it she looks back, more with distaste than longing, to her Kentucky childhood. 'When I left home,' she recalls, 'my brother said : it will be wonderful if you make a success of life, then you can follow the races.' It was not quite what she had in mind, but images from those early days often surfaced.*

Still I remember the old race tracks, before Keeneland was built, before the barns burned and the horses screamed all night in their prisons. A pastoral quality then, something theatrical and marginal, like the coming of the circus. The lustrous afternoons, faded blue paled by sunlight, the soft May air. The tracks at dawn, the early sun, the tranquil curve of the empty grandstands.

Near the end of the afternoon the important race is finally run. The purity of the dawn is forgotten. The dogwood and the lilac droop in the chill. And then the stress of the race, the pain and the pleasure of the outrageous effort are finally consecrated in a few moments. The sacrificial power of the horse and its

Faustian contract with the jockey – something can be learned from that. A *tristesse* falls down upon the scene, down on the old memory. The horses are led away to their rest, their feelings about the race they have run unknown to us.

Perhaps it is true that being from where I am I was born a gambler. And as the gambler in Dostoevsky's great story says: 'It is true that only one out of a hundred wins, but what is that to me?'

*Kingsclere is on the edge of some of the best training country in the world, that magic tilted triangle whose apex is Didcot and whose southern base runs between Marlborough and Andover. Within it lie the establishments of Fred Winter and the Walwyns, Tim Forster and Henry Candy, the Baldings, to name only a few. The village of Lambourn is at the heart of it, nestling under miles of rolling downland and open sky. John Betjeman, though he married a Field Marshal's daughter, is no great man of the Turf, but his poem 'Upper Lambourn' is an evocative tribute to the racing country in which he himself lived for many years:*

> Up the ash-tree climbs the ivy,
>     Up the ivy climbs the sun,
> With a twenty-thousand pattering
>     Has a valley breeze begun,
> Feathery ash, neglected elder,
>     Shift the shade and make it run –
>
> Shift the shade toward the nettles,
>     And the nettles set it free
> To streak the stained Cararra headstone
>     Where, in nineteen-twenty-three,
> He who trained a hundred winners
>     Paid the Final Entrance Fee.

## SOME RACECOURSES

Leathery limbs of Upper Lambourn,
  Leathery skin from sun and wind,
Leathery breeches, spreading stables,
  Shining saddles left behind –
To the down the string of horses
  Moving out of sight and mind.

Feathery ash in leathery Lambourn
  Waves above the sarsen stone,
And Edwardian plantations
  So coniferously moan
As to make the swelling downland,
  Far-surrounding, seem their own.

From *Old Lights for New Chancels*, 1940

# Occasions & Episodes

The bell rang and Brown Jack and Solatium entered the Straight well clear of any other runner. It was certain then that one of the two would win. Solatium, on the rails, hung on most gallantly to Brown Jack. Indeed, he hung on so long that the suspense to me became almost unbearable.

Solatium belongs to a great friend of mine, but how I hoped his horse would fall away beaten so that Brown Jack could win! And then slowly but surely Brown Jack and Donoghue began to draw away; at first by inches and then by feet, and then, quite close to the winning post, they were clear and the race was over. Brown Jack and his friend won by two lengths from Solatium, who had run a most gallant race and had been ridden as ably as a horse could be ridden by Caldwell. Some of the runners were struggling past the winning post after Brown Jack had been pulled up and was returning to the Paddock, and Mail Fist received a special cheer as he went by long after his friend.

I have never seen such a sight anywhere, and especially never at Ascot, as I was privileged to see when Brown Jack went past the winning post. Eminently respectable old ladies in the Royal Enclosure gathered up their skirts and began, with such dignity as they could command in their excitement, to make the best of their way as quickly as they could towards the place where Brown Jack and Donoghue would return after the race. Hats were raised in the air in every enclosure and there were cheers from all parts of the course. Such a scene could be witnessed only in this country, and it has never in my time been witnessed here in such intensity. The unsaddling enclosure to which Brown Jack was returning for the sixth time after winning this race was surrounded many times deep. Crowds were waiting round the gateway leading from the course to the Enclosure. Police made a lane for the triumphant pair, Brown Jack and Donoghue. The trainer, Ivor Anthony, as shy and bashful as ever, had already gone into the unsaddling enclosure where he was standing stroking his chin and trying to look unconcerned: he had been too nervous to watch the race, and had sat alone under the trees in the paddock until the great roar of cheering told him all was well.

And then at last Brown Jack came in. He looked to the right and to the left as he walked through the lane from the course to his own enclosure. His ears were pricked and he knew full well what was happening and what had happened. He was being patted on both sides from head to tail as he made his progress. 'Half his tail was pulled out', Sir Harold Wernher told me afterwards. And then when he got to the gateway to his own enclosure he stood still. Donoghue tried to persuade him to go in, but he would not move. His ears were pricked and he was most certainly watching the people still pouring into the Paddock to see his return. He would not disappoint them. When he thought that all had arrived he walked in quietly and received the congratulations of his owner, his owner's wife, and his trainer. Donoghue, in some wonderful way, wormed his way through the people to the weighing room, and after that came the end.

*That comes from* Brown Jack (*1934*) *by R. C. Lyle, after Brown Jack had won the Queen Alexandra Stakes at Royal Ascot for the sixth year running. Brown Jack, one of the most popular of all racehorses and also one of the sleepiest, died in 1948 aged twenty-four.*

I call to mind several amusing episodes in the racing
career of King Edward. I was on the racecourse side
that morning of the Craven week when Persimmon was
galloped alongside the flat and badly beaten by two
Platers. The Prince's cob was standing by, and sup-
posed, like all well-trained cobs at Newmarket, to never
dream of moving off, but the defeat of Persimmon
appeared to upset him badly, and away he went across
the Heath kicking up his heels and pursued by Marsh
and Lord Marcus Beresford on their hacks. A tout
eventually caught him and he was brought back, but it
was a disconcerting morning's work.

There was one occasion, after his Coronation, when
King Edward had reached Newmarket by train, and,
through some misunderstanding, a carriage was not
there to meet him, whereupon he got into an ordinary
fly and drove off, with whoever was in attendance, to
the Jockey Club rooms. It is almost inconceivable that
anybody at Newmarket should not know the King by
sight, but that driver did not, and when his Majesty
got down and walked hastily to the rooms, the man ran
after him, under the impression that he was going to be
'bilked'.

William Allison, *Memories of Men and Horses*, 1922

*Owners tend to be more often disappointed with expensive*
*purchases than pleased with cheap ones. The circumstances*
*in which the Duke of Portland acquired the great St Simon*
*— no less than those in which the Duke of Devonshire*
*agreed to buy Park Top as a favour to his trainer who had*
*bred her — are an encouraging exception. He described*
*them in* The Field *in 1923 :*

St Simon (Galopin – St Angela) was foaled in 1881 and
was bred by Prince Batthyany. My first sight of him
was in the following year, when he was at Barrow's
Paddocks at Newmarket. On that occasion I did not

notice that he was an animal of any particular quality, nor did I then imagine that he would subsequently come into my possession, and develop into the wonderful horse that he proved to be.

It was in 1883 that my association with him began. In April of that year, during the First Spring Meeting, there occurred the tragically sudden death of Prince Batthyany, on the Two Thousand Guineas Day, about half an hour before the race. . . .

In consequence of this sad event, Prince Batthyany's horses were sold at the ensuing July Meeting, and I asked Mathew Dawson's advice as to buying Fulmen, who had been a prominent two-year-old, but had not run as a three-year-old, owing to the Prince's death. His trainer was John Dawson, Mathew's brother.

Mat accompanied me to the stables to inspect the horses, and we each thought Fulmen a very nice animal; he then proposed that we should look at the others, and in the box next to that in which Fulmen stood, we found a brown two-year-old colt called St Simon.

Mat remarked (and I agreed): 'This is quite a likely-looking animal.' We noticed that its hock had been dressed with some white substance. I asked Mat if he thought it had a curb. He passed his hand over the place, and said he did not think there was anything that mattered in the least, adding that the white stuff smelt more like paint than blister. At the same time he jokingly said: 'I will pull John's leg over this.' As we walked home, I told Mat that I would bid up to 4,500 guineas for Fulmen, and his answer was: 'I think you should get him for that, but if you don't do so, have a bid for the two-year-old, and in the meantime I will try to find out something about him from my brother John.'

The next morning Mat accompanied me to the sale, and Fulmen was knocked down at 500 guineas in excess of my bid, very fortunately for me as it turned out.

St Simon was then led into the ring, and Mat asked me how much he should bid. I answered: 'Go on, and I will tell you when to stop.' The result was that the horse became mine for 1,600 guineas. I have heard, but I do not know if it is true, that the late Duke of Hamilton was the penultimate bidder. I have, however, been assured by Mr Alfred Brisco, who at that time was an owner of racehorses, that the under-bidder was Sir Charles Day Rose.

We then found John Dawson, whom Mat had been unable to see before the sale, and Mat asked him to tell us all he knew about the colt, and whether he was worth the money. John answered: 'Yes, I should think he ought to be worth about that price, but I really don't know a great deal about him. I tried him in the spring, before the Prince died, with Rout, a five-year-old, belonging to Gen. Owen Williams, and he beat Rout easily; but owing to an accident, I have been unable to run Rout since, so that I really don't know what the trial is worth.' Rout, I may say, shortly after this won the Prince of Wales's Cup, a good Five-Furlong Handicap at Kempton Park, carrying 8 st. 2 lb.

After this interview with John Dawson, Mat made me a courtly bow, and said: 'I think I may congratulate Your Grace on a good morning's work.' Subsequent events showed that, as usual, the dear old fellow was quite right.

The next morning I saw the horse at exercise, and he was not in anything like condition – in fact, he was as fat as a bull. Mat sent him a canter for our inspection, and we were both perfectly disgusted with his action. He appeared to move more like a rabbit than a horse, and could not apparently stride over a straw. When I returned to breakfast, my friend, Lord Enniskillen, told me that he had seen the famous trainer, Robert

Peck, who said he had heard that Mat and I were much disappointed with our purchase, and if this was so, he would gladly take him off my hands for 2,000 guineas, thus giving me an immediate profit of 400 guineas. I answered Lord Enniskillen that I was much obliged for Mr Peck's offer, but as I had the greatest respect in the world for Mr Peck's judgment, I thought no better advice to retain the horse could be given to me than the offer he had made. If he was worth 2,000 guineas to Peck, he was certainly worth that to me, and consequently nothing would induce me to part with him.

I have no certain knowledge why St Simon was not entered for the Derby or the St Leger by Prince Batthyany, but I believe that his dam was seventeen or eighteen years old when she gave birth to him, and that she had not previously bred any animal of much racing ability, and perhaps it may have been for that reason that Prince Batthyany did not think it worth while to enter this colt very heavily.

*Few racing books fail to provide interesting cross-references of one kind or another. The prize-fighting Jimmy Carney who appears in Jack Leach's memoirs is mentioned by Lambton in connection with an awkward incident that took place at Nottingham. Lambton was*

riding a horse called *Westwood* in a three-horse race. *Westwood* was a well-known bolter and no sooner had they hit the front than *Westwood* set off for some spiked railings bordering the course. By the time Lambton got him back under control the race was lost. On returning to the paddock, Lambton was abused 'by a great big fat brute' and jumping off his horse he gave him two cuts across the face with his whip. There was instant pandemonium among the local roughs, known as the 'Nottingham Lambs', and though Fred Archer and several others came to Lambton's rescue matters were looking dangerous. 'I suddenly saw some of my opponents going down like ninepins. This was the work of Jim Carney, ex-champion of England . . . and when he hit his man, down he went'. It was a narrow escape.

It is typical of Lambton that he should write sympathetically of Horatio Bottomley, after his disgrace.

Although he prided himself on being a great financier, I believe him to have been one of the worst. I remember one of his secretaries saying to me 'Oh, the Guvnor is a child about money, he never has any and never will have any'.

About racing matters, Lambton observes, 'although Bottomley had a large stud of very bad horses, he was supremely ignorant and lost heavily'.

Bottomley in his memoirs *Bottomley's Book* devotes a chapter to 'Racing Reflections'. His horses don't seem to have been quite as moderate as Lambton makes out, though he obviously bought them by the dozen and raced them recklessly. He won the Cesarewitch, the Stewards' Cup, and the Great Sandown Steeplechase among many other lesser races. About his failures he writes with rueful modesty:

I have had a fair share of disappointments. Like many another young owner, I thought I would begin by winning the Derby; and, accordingly, I approached Mr John Porter, the veteran Kingsclere trainer, with a view to the purchase of Hawfinch, a rising three-year-old which had astounded the racing world by running away towards the end of the previous season with the Dewhurst Plate – one of the most important two-year-old events at Newmarket. I need not here go into intricate questions of pedigree; sufficient to say that the horse, duly entered for the Derby, appeared to possess about the best chance of the year, and so, after a veterinary examination, I gave Mr Porter £5,000 for it; and throughout the winter and the spring it was favourite in the betting for what is called the Blue Riband of the Turf. That it did not win was, and always will be to my mind, no fault of the horse. Despite the warnings of my trainer – J. H. Batho – I'm afraid that, in racing phrase, I 'left the race at home'. I wanted to see a Derby trial every time I went to the training grounds, with the result that on Derby Day itself the poor animal was more fit for the kennels than the race. As a matter of fact, I was advised not to start it, but the public were 'on' to a man, and I decided to give them a run for their money. And, after all, the horse just missed getting into the first three, or, in technical language, being 'placed' – which satisfied us all that under normal conditions he was beyond all doubt the 'best of his year'. I had, early in the betting, taken £10,000 to £2,500 about him, but I lost the money with complacency – for I had a 'plater' named Splendour, which immediately after the Derby had been run, brought me off a six to one chance to £500, so that I went home a 'monkey' in pocket!

*Not only did Bottomley run Hawfinch into the ground but he insisted on running Wargrave in another race the day after he won the Cesarewitch.*

*Julian Symons in his biography of Bottomley (1955) comments on his foolhardiness, as well as observing that there was never any scandal attached to his racing activities. 'On the contrary, bookmakers welcomed his arrival on the course and vendors of horses regarded him as a pigeon to be plucked'. He continues,*

Yet though he knew surprisingly little about horses, Bottomley was passionately fond of them, not merely as potential money-makers, and was most reluctant to part with any of them. The lesser lights in his stable were constantly winning selling plates ... and Bottomley would always buy them in, often at ridiculously high prices. Adansi, which won him twenty races, most of them selling plates, cost him a fortune at auctions.

*Sadly, after his various bankruptcies, and subsequent imprisonment, all his horses had to be either given away or sold. The last lot of twenty went for less than £2,000.*

*John Hislop has a good story about Bottomley on his first day in prison. On his morning exercise he espied Captain Peel, an old racecourse acquaintance sent down for swindling, cutting the grass. Bottomley called out to him as he passed, 'Hullo, still at the Turf, I see'.*

# *Acknowledgements*

For their help in making suggestions for this book I am indebted
to many people, most especially to those who wrote in out of the
blue in answer to my letter in *The Sporting Life*. John Hislop, for
many years the *Observer*'s racing correspondent when I was its
cricket correspondent, was typically generous with ideas. Without
Michael Seth-Smith's kindness in making me free of his library
and getting extracts from books copied my task would have been
doubly difficult. I have relied greatly, as anyone in these circumstances must do for the facts, on *The Biographical Encyclopaedia
of British Flat Racing* (1978) by Roger Mortimer, Richard Onslow,
and Peter Willett, on Roger Longrigg's *The History of Horse
Racing* (1972), and on *The History of Steeplechasing* (1966), by
Michael Seth-Smith, Peter Willett, Roger Mortimer, and John
Lawrence. The best anthologies on racing that I know are *The
Racing Man's Bedside Book* (1969), edited by Dick Francis and
John Welcome, and *The Horseman's Companion* (1967), edited by
Dorian Williams. They have been always at my elbow, but I have
gone to some pains to avoid taking their ground.

The editor and publishers gratefully acknowledge permission
to use copyright material in this book:

Hilaire Belloc: Extract from *More Peers*. Reprinted by permission
of Duckworth & Co. Ltd.

John Betjeman: Extract from *Old Lights for New Chancels*. Reprinted by permission of John Murray (Publishers) Ltd.

Horatio Bottomley: Extract from *Bottomley's Book*. Reprinted by
permission of Odhams Books Ltd.

D. W. E. Brock: Extract from *The Racing Man's Weekend Book*
(1949). Reprinted by permission of Seeley Service & Co. Ltd.

Roy Campbell: Extract from *Adamastor* (1930). Reprinted by permission of Faber & Faber Ltd.

Andrew Devonshire: Extracts from *Park Top* (1976). Reprinted
by permission of London Magazine Editions.

W. G. C. Frith: Extract from *The History of the Calcutta Race
Club*. Reprinted by permission of The Royal Calcutta Turf
Club.

Quintin Gilbey: Passages from *Champions All* (1971). Reprinted
by permission of Hutchinson & Co.

Clive Graham: Extract from *Hyperion* (1967). Reprinted by permission of J. A. Allen & Co. Ltd.

Elizabeth Hardwick: Extract from *Sleepless Nights* (1979). Reprinted by permission of Weidenfeld & Nicolson Ltd.

Ernest Hemingway: Extract from *A Moveable Feast* (1965). Reprinted by permission of Jonathan Cape Ltd.

John Hislop: Extracts from *The Turf* (1948). Reprinted by permission of William Collins. Passage from *Far From a Gentleman* (1954). Reprinted by permission of Michael Joseph Ltd. Extract from *The Brigadier* (1973). Reprinted by permission of Secker & Warburg Ltd. Extract from *Anything But a Soldier* (1965). Reprinted by permission of the author.

Geoffrey Holloway: Extract from 'Oedipus at Newmarket'. Reprinted by permission of London Magazine.

George Lambton: Extract from *Men and Horses I Have Known* (1924). Reprinted by permission of Thornton Butterworth and J. A. Allen & Co. Ltd.

Jack Leach: Extracts from *Sods I have Cut on the Turf* (1961). Reprinted by permission of J. A. Allen & Co. Ltd.

Roger Longrigg: Extracts from *The History of Horse Racing* (1972). Reprinted by permission of Macmillan, London and Basingstoke.

R. C. Lyle: Extract from *Brown Jack* (1934). Reprinted by permission of Putnam & Co. Ltd. Extract from *The Aga Khan's Horses* (1938). Reprinted by permission of Putnam & Co. Ltd.

John Masefield: Extract from 'An Epilogue'. Reprinted by permission of The Society of Authors.

Prince Monolulu: Extract from *I Gotta Horse* (1950). Reprinted by permission of Hurst & Blackett Ltd.

Roger Mortimer: Extract from *Anthony Mildmay* (1955). Reprinted by permission of the author. Extracts from *British Flat Racing* (1978). Reprinted by permission of Macdonald & Jane's Ltd.

Leslie Norris: Extract from 'Ormonde' (1980). Reprinted by permission of the author and J. M. Dent & Sons Ltd.

John Oaksey: Extract from *The Story of Mill Reef* (1974). Reprinted by permission of the author and Michael Joseph Ltd.

Richard Onslow: Extracts from *British Flat Racing* (1978). Reprinted by permission of Macdonald & Jane's Ltd.

Duke of Portland: Extract from *Memories of Racing and Hunting* (1935). Reprinted by permission of Faber & Faber Ltd.

Ezra Pound: Extract from 'Near Perigord' in *Selected Poems* (1940). Reprinted by permission of Faber & Faber Ltd. Extract from 'The Garden'. Reprinted by permission of Faber & Faber Ltd.

P. E. Ricketts: Extract from *Flat Racing* (1940). Reprinted by permission of the author.

Alan Ross: Extracts from *Death Valley* (1980). Reprinted by permission of London Magazine Editions.

## ACKNOWLEDGEMENTS

Michael Seth-Smith: Extract from *The History of Steeplechasing*
(1966). Reprinted by permission of Michael Joseph Ltd. Extract from *Bred for the Purple* (1969). Reprinted by permission
of the author. Extract from *Steve* (1974). Reprinted by permission of Faber & Faber Ltd.

Julian Symons: Extract from the *Biography of Horatio Bottomley*
(1955). Reprinted by permission of the author.

Wray Vamplew: Extract from *The Turf* (1976). Reprinted by permission of Allen Lane.

John Welcome: Extract from *Fred Archer* (1967). Reprinted by
permission of Faber & Faber Ltd.

Philip Welsh: Extracts from *Stable Rat* (1979). Reprinted by permission of Eyre Methuen Ltd.

Peter Willett: Extracts from *British Flat Racing* (1978). Reprinted
by permission of Macdonald & Jane's Ltd.

Kenneth Young: Extract from *Harry, Lord Rosebery* (1974). Reprinted by permission of Hodder & Stoughton Ltd.

While every effort has been made to secure permission, we may
have failed in a few cases to trace the copyright holder. We
apologize for any apparent negligence.

The illustrations in this book were taken from Earl of Suffolk
and Berkshire, W. G. Craven, Arthur Coventry, and Alfred E. T.
Watson, *Racing and Steeple-Chasing* (London, 1886).

# Index